STEPPING
INTO
THE IMPOSSIBLE

THE STORY OF
HEALING ON THE STREETS

MARK MARX

RIVER
PUBLISHING

River Publishing & Media Ltd
Barham Court
Teston
Maidstone
Kent
ME18 5BZ
United Kingdom

info@river-publishing.co.uk

ISBN 978-1-908393-05-0
Cover design by www.spiffingcovers.com
Printed by Bell & Bain Ltd, Glasgow

CONTENTS

DEDICATION

Linda, Joshua, Timothy and Jordan – we faced giants and shared the adventure; we stepped into the impossible together. There are many stories that could not be told, but this one is for you, with love.

ACKNOWLEDGEMENTS

Lynn and Mick Elias – you were a God send. Thank you for your love and patience, your expertise and timely help, without which this book could not have been written.

Rose Lynas – thank you for casting an expert eye over the manuscript and for your wise advice.

Caroline Mara, Alan Scott, Jamie Watters – thank you for your valuable input.

Tim Pettingale, River Publishing – thank you for your incredible patience, kingdom mindedness and help.

WHAT OTHERS ARE SAYING...

"Mark Marx is carrying something from God. He is a man of tenacious faith; a compelling practitioner in a world of theoreticians. After so many years out on the streets in all weathers, simply 'doing the stuff', witnessing miracles in answer to prayer and provoking others around the world to rediscover the simple things of faith, Mark's message deserves to be heard. I defy you to read this book without shaking your head in amazement, without muttering 'Wow!', without hatching your own plans to step into the impossible wherever you live."
Pete Greig, 24-7 Prayer & Alpha International

"A fascinating, stimulating and thought-provoking book about the Healing on the Streets ministry. A powerful challenge to the Church to bring the miraculous back into its outreach."
Revd Canon J. John, The Philo Trust

"Wow! Buckle up and strap yourself in for an adventure ride filled with the highs and lows of a life surrendered to Jesus. This story should inspire and provoke you to give yourself to the One who will take smallness and exchange it for deep and awesome! Mark Marx is a man who knows Jesus. This alone is enough. But the testimony of his encounter with a living God will light a fire in your belly. May God let that fire burn bright in all of us!"
Danielle Strickland, speaker, author and Salvation Army leader, Edmonton, Canada.

"Mark is a man of great faith, radical risk, deep connection to Jesus, and steadfast compassion for those beyond the walls of the Church. The way he ministers healing and lets everyone else

in on 'how to do it' exactly represents the heart of the Father and is part of the legacy we treasure in the Vineyard. As the wild adventure of Causeway Coast Vineyard has unfolded, Mark and Linda have been right at the core, raising the bar of risk; faithful stewards of the 'more' of the Kingdom. This book is the beautiful and powerful story of how Healing on the Streets came to be, and how you too can partner with the Holy Spirit as He broods over your city, your town, your neighbourhood – the mission field right within your reach."
Kathryn Scott, Worship leader/songwriter

"Whilst making my movies I've met a lot of evangelists and I've filmed a lot of wild stuff. When I first met Mark, an unassuming man of quiet disposition and gentle spirit, I had no idea that I was about to embark on one of the most impossible adventures I'd ever filmed. It is no joke, then, that this book is titled *Stepping Into the Impossible*, because that's what Mark does every day. The thing I like most about Mark, and indeed this book, is the fact that he's a normal guy. He's not a weirdo. He's not a sensationalist. He's just a man who loves Jesus, and more importantly TRUSTS Jesus to do what He says He'll do. In this book you'll find out how God took a normal guy to abnormal places, but you'll also discover how the invitation is waiting for you to do the impossible as well, in a no nonsense, gentle, and easy-going way. Mark Marx is legit. And his book is too."
Darren Wilson, Director, *Finger of God, Furious Love, Father of Lights* and *Holy Ghost*

"I can think of few Christians in this generation who have done more to equip the saints than Mark Marx. *Stepping Into the Impossible* shows what one man can achieve for the King and

his Kingdom when filled with the Holy Spirit and taking God at his Word. It had me laughing out loud with unbridled joy at the goodness of God in transforming broken lives. An extraordinary account from an extraordinary man who knows his extraordinary God."
Simon Ponsonby, Pastor of Theology, St Aldates, Oxford

"When I first met Mark Marx I expected him to rip open his shirt and reveal a big 'S' on his chest. But he is way too humble for that! The big 'S' he packs is the Spirit of God. He walks in great power, but in even greater love and grace. He is one of my heroes! This book will blow your mind, but equip you to go out and do the same as you've read in its pages. Brace for impact, but resistance is futile."
Robby Dawkins, Author of *Do What Jesus Did*, Pastor, Equipper and fellow Power Evangelist

"Mark Marx and I have shared some amazing times together on the streets of India. This book is not another 'how-to' manual, it is the story behind the story. What develops a life of risk and radical faith? What sustains a life in Christ beyond the miracles and moments that seem to define so many other ministries and movements? Mark has once again put his heart out there for us all to see and I believe it will bless many who long to live in the kind of obedience that Jesus is searching for in those who call him Lord. This book will motivate you and convict you in all the right ways. Don't miss this chance to peek behind the scenes of one man's life and get some new tools along the way."
Jake Hamilton, Musician and Lead Catalyst for Transcendent Media

"Be warned – you will not be able to put this book down once you start it! It will fascinate, inspire and challenge you. Once again, we have cause to be very grateful to Mark for this wonderful contribution to our grasp of healing, and it will be for the benefit and blessing of the whole Body of Christ."
John Mumford, National Leader, Vineyard Churches UK & Ireland

"*Stepping Into the Impossible* is both faith building and practical. Mark has been faithfully doing this stuff for years. He lives what he teaches. This is authentic and accessible. Buy it, study it and do it!"
Mike Pilavachi, Soul Survivor

FOREWORD

Step into the impossible.

The greatest stories are told by ordinary heroes; people so gripped by the beauty and generosity of God that they gave their whole lives. Mark Marx is one of my heroes.

Mark's passionate pursuit of God is quiet, gentle, brimming with authority. His great joy is equipping the Church to witness the kingdom among the people.

This book opens up the story, gives us a glimpse into the man. It invites us on a journey.

I am inspired by Mark's journey. He has modelled adventurous authority, true humility. He has done so in the context of community. Each January Mark invites me to breakfast. In those moments together he reaffirms his submission to leadership, his commitment to local church. Those moments are intense ... and rare. Often people with outstanding gifting have difficulty submitting. Not Mark. His priority is the local church; his passion is releasing the whole Church to step into the impossible.

Stepping into the impossible reminds us that we can't impress our cities into life. We can immerse them in the life to come. We can bring back life. We must bring back life – it's our assignment, for which we will be held accountable. Developing life-giving churches at the centre of the city involves more than creating irresistible environments marked by excellence and service. Any human industry can accomplish those goals. Life-giving churches are defined by the life of another world; they are steeped in the impossible.

God has promised joy to the world. He is waiting for Kingdom servants to drag the promise to the surface. The capacity for joy in the city is accelerated through believers immersed in the presence and power of God. When they show up there is great joy in the city. Our communities are not hard to reach. They are just hard to reach when we stay in church. Everything changes as we step into the impossible.

I love this book.

I love its invitation to adventure ... to more. I love its risk-taking stories, its revelatory paradigms, its refusal to settle. In these pages, Mark moves us beyond phenomena in meetings to releasing power on the streets. He invites each of us to show up in our community and to demonstrate the Kingdom with compassionate authority. He challenges us to recognise that the Spirit was not given for better meetings but for broken humanity.

Mostly I love the book because I know and love Mark. I am honoured to count him as a friend. I have watched him handle failure and favour, brokenness and breakthrough with relentless faith. I have witnessed first hand his faith stir a local church and then gate crash an unsuspecting community. I have marvelled as he has delivered the demonised on planes; stood open mouthed as deformities have straightened; looked on bleary-eyed as he has prayed during the watches of the night; and more than once have wrestled with unbelief as multiple stories of cancer being healed have unfolded.

Like many others I have been won by Mark's ferocious gentleness; his tenacious hope; his invitation into the story unfolding beyond the walls of the Church. He has challenged, provoked and stretched me. His life journey has led me to the awareness that the next great move of God is not a movement IN the Church but a movement OF the Church as she steps into the impossible. I pray reading this book does the same for you.

Alan Scott
Lead Pastor, Causeway Coast Vineyard

1

EARLY YEARS

When I look back over my life I am astounded at what has unfolded and how, despite such very unpromising beginnings, God has done something that is truly remarkable with my life – something that social status, education, wealth, all those things that the world holds so dear, could never do. There is nothing I would trade for the adventure of living a life following the leading of the Holy Spirit.

The story of Healing on the Streets is not my story, it is not the story of Mark Marx. It is the story of the Holy Spirit and what he can and will do with the man, woman or child who simply believes and obeys. Obedience hasn't always been an easy option nor, from a human point of view, has it always appeared to be the best course of action, but choosing to believe and to follow Jesus regardless has turned out to be both exciting and deeply satisfying. I am discovering that my life now is having an impact way beyond what I could ever have hoped or dreamed and I am convinced that the best years still lie ahead.

I was born in Cape Town, South Africa, in 1957 to a Chinese father and a Jewish mother. I took my mother's name of Marx, as my parents were unable to marry. The apartheid system in South Africa at the time, prevented all mixed race unions. Under The Prohibition of Mixed Marriages Act of 1949, which was one of the first pieces of legislation passed by the then ruling National Party, and a further Immorality Act passed a year later, not just marriage, but any extramarital sexual relationship between people of different races was completely outlawed.

My grandfather, who was a Chinese government official, had fled to South Africa via Taiwan in the early 1900s. The destruction and havoc wreaked in China by the Opium Wars and then the Boxer Rebellion no doubt influenced his decision to seek a better life elsewhere and he eventually settled in Port Elizabeth, which is where my father was born and grew up.

The family made a living through running a small grocery business, but that business soon ran into trouble because of some black market dealings my grandfather had entered into. It wasn't long before the authorities caught up with him and he subsequently lost his trading licence.

In an attempt to start afresh he relocated his family to Cape Town. There, in order to get alongside the authorities, my grandfather encouraged my father to drink with the police and regularly provided him with bottles of whisky and brandy expressly for this purpose. Thus it was that my father had already become an alcoholic by the time I came into the world.

My grandfather's strategy of getting around the law was an utter failure and his shady past caught up with him again in Cape Town. Since by then my father knew no other way of making money except in the grocery trade, he decided that his best option was to emigrate and try and make a life somewhere else.

When I was just three-and-a-half years old, my father told my mother that we were going to England. My grandmother, sensing that the prospects of a life abroad with my father looked bleak, eventually dissuaded my mother from going, but my father refused to leave me behind.

I was his firstborn and only son, and my father was devoted to me. He was an intelligent and gentle man and I adored him. The earliest memory I have is of him shaking a bush, chameleons dropping out of it, and my father picking one up and giving it to me to play with.

Since my mother had been deterred from leaving and my father could not be persuaded to change his plans, at that young age I was separated from my mother never to see her again. In the February of 1961 my father and I boarded the RMS Edinburgh Castle and made the 6,000 mile journey from Cape Town to the port of Southampton.

Once in England I grew up in the East End of London within an extended family of aunts and uncles. I was enrolled into a Catholic Primary School and, as I look back now, I realise it was there that I began to sense an awakening of my heart to the existence of God.

I can remember going with my school to services in the Catholic church of St Anthony in Forest Gate. Right above us, as we went in through the main entrance, hung a large crucifix which I found completely arresting. To me as a child it seemed massive and the image of Jesus hanging on the cross was haunting. The anticipation of being greeted by this crucified Christ every time I walked through the doors of the church filled me with awe.

Inside the church I would wonder about some of my classmates who would go into the confessional booth each week. I wasn't allowed to go in, although I never really discovered why. I can only surmise that it was because the teachers knew that my mother and father weren't married. But whatever it was, something precluded me from being allowed to go in and that gave rise to many questions in my mind. I once asked a teacher why it is that you have to put your hands together when you pray, but no one seemed able to give me any satisfactory answers.

One teacher, however, would regularly give us communion in the classroom. She gave all of us children these little round wafers to eat. Extraordinarily, many years later, I was sitting on a park bench and there was an elderly lady sitting next to me. She turned to me and said,

"Mark?"

I nodded and looked at her, but I didn't recognise her at all.

"I thought it was you!" she exclaimed.

And she began to explain that she'd been my teacher in primary school. She asked me what I was doing with my life now, and when I told her, the tears began to flow, because she was the one who'd given me communion and had been praying for me for many years. She recognised me from when I was a little boy and I was blown away.

After primary school I boarded at Tavistock Hall Preparatory school in Sussex. My aunt was an influential and wealthy woman and she had taken it upon herself to see to my education.

Because of the family business, my grandfather had discouraged his other children from completing their education, but with my aunt he had made an exception, and she was the only member of the family to complete their studies. As a result she had prospered.

When I was at Tavistock Hall I somehow got into the choir at All Saints, Waldron. Of course, you could earn money being a choir boy, but I think even back then there was something in me that just wanted to be in church. I had some searching questions and I wanted to know where I was from and why I was here. There was a sense of God, but no real understanding. I had no frame of reference at that time and no one was giving me any answers.

When we were all robed up with our gowns and ruffs, we choirboys looked a pretty amazing bunch. We might have been from another era, but as we waited together in a small ante-room for the time to come for us to process into the main church, I could feel there was something different about this place, compared to how I felt everywhere else. I didn't know what it was, even though I was very much aware of it. Now, of course, looking back I know that I had encountered the Holy Spirit there.

I enjoyed my four years at Tavistock Hall, before being enrolled in the much tougher Gordon Boys military boarding school in Surrey. The school was named after General Gordon of Khartoum and even the regular army of the day would have said that it was hardcore, old-school army life they were drilling into us.

I would wake up each morning to reveille and had to barrack my bed before school. It was incredibly tough. One thing it taught me though was how to look after myself. I was able to sew a button on a shirt at any rate!

Our house was subjected to a full inspection every Sunday, which meant that Saturdays were spent cleaning and polishing the wooden floors to perfection and making sure everything was spick and span. There wasn't to be a speck of dust anywhere in sight.

We also had to clean and press our regimental uniforms – our dark tunics and trousers of Gordon tartan. Our brass Glengarry badges and the brass buttons on our tunics had to be polished so that they shone like glass. Even our shoes had to be spit and polished so that you could see your reflection in them – and not just the uppers, but especially the bridge between the heel and the sole. The one thing that most concerned us when we were marching on parade on a Sunday was that someone might step on our shoes and we'd have to repeat the whole spit-and-polish routine to make them look like glass again.

As the Gordon Boys School was a Church of England school, attendance at church on a Sunday was compulsory. Many of the boys were choosing to get confirmed, but although I had an interest in religious education, I wasn't yet persuaded of its truth.

The school had a library of ancient books which were beautifully illustrated with pictures of Jerusalem and the Holy Land. I loved poring over these old volumes, studying the pictures and I found the stories so captivating. I think the padre could see that there was a drawing of my heart to God, because one day he called me, along with two other boys who were bucking the trend of confirmation, into his study, and he made a really heartfelt plea for us all to go through confirmation.

But I couldn't respond because I couldn't do anything I wasn't utterly convinced about. If I did something, it had to be true for me. And I know he was so disappointed. But I'm sure he is rejoicing now, and I truly believe his prayers must have helped play a part in my getting to where I am now. It's amazing to look back and be able to see God's hand on my life right the way through.

My best subject at school was art and I was always drawing and painting. Being creative, I decided to go to art college when I finished school, but having had such a strict five years at military boarding school and then being let loose into art college was like going from one extreme to the other. From excessive discipline to the absence of all discipline was too much for me. I wasn't equipped to handle it sensibly.

After four years at art college I qualified as a graphic designer. While working for a fashion company in Oxford Street I painted a mural in a hairdressing salon for a friend's boss during one of my holiday breaks. From the exposure and success that came from that I launched a business as an interior decorating specialist. I loved my work and in the ensuing seven years I did a self-apprenticeship in wood graining, marbelising and specialised paint finishes.

I got the most amazing break with the famous architect, Charles Jencks, and alongside some other very eminent people I did commission work for him at his London home for an exhibition of furniture. It was his furniture exhibition in Covent Garden that helped launch my interior decorating career and on the back of that I secured commissions decorating wine bars, restaurants and the homes of the rich and famous.

All this time my father was steadily getting worse. As his only child, I felt a sense of responsibility towards him and did my level best to stop him drinking. I knew where he hid his whisky and I'd get hold of it and pour it down the drain. But all we ever did was end up fighting over it and then he'd just get hold of another bottle anyway.

The last thing I heard the doctor say to my father was that if he didn't stop smoking and drinking he was going to die. I was so angry at the fact that I'd fought for years to try and keep him from harming himself, that at that moment I gave up. I went and to him and told him just that:

"I give up on you! I don't know why I've bothered doing all these things to try and help you. I might just as well have drunk myself and taken drugs and gone down the same path you have."

I left his house and I went to my workshop in Stratford which was above Bobby Moore's old pub, and then I went into the pub and got drunk. In the morning I went back to my father's home only to find that he had died in the very position where I'd left him when I said, "I give up on you."

My world fell apart with the death of my father. I had watched someone I loved with all my heart kill himself at the age of fifty-five. It was an awful thing to find him and I felt extremely guilty because of my final words to him.

I sank into a terrible depression. I didn't know who to turn to or how to express my feelings.

I would go to the pub, having hundreds of pounds in one pocket and a bottle of vodka in the other, get drunk on beer and spirits, then head into central London to go to a night club – only to wake up and find myself on a train outside of London with hardly anything in my pocket. I once woke up on some railway station concourse with a homeless man slapping me in the face as I came to, while at the same time trying to prise the watch from my wrist.

My world had crumbled around me and I thought my life was over. The money had gone, I stopped working, and my life went into a downward spiral of guilt, pain and hopelessness.

I was thirty years old.

2

ENCOUNTERING JESUS

When I was at art college I made a good friend called Paul. Neither of us were Christians, although I think that Paul might have had some Christian background.

While I was working as an interior decorator, Paul had an encounter with God and he wanted to tell me about Jesus, so one of the first things he did was to invite me to church. He wasn't going to readily take "no" for an answer, yet the more persistent he became, the more resistant I became.

Being such a good friend, Paul wanted to help me, because at the time I was pretty broken. I'd lost my father to alcohol and I'd never really known my mother, and Paul felt that Jesus could help me.

I kept refusing. Since my art college days, I wore my thick, dark hair very long. I was this arty, creative-looking type, but with a strange sense of dress, and I really thought that church would be an uncomfortable place for me to go to because I would never fit in.

The image I had of church came not from any prior experience on my part, but from the jokey kind of Christianity that TV poked fun at. The image portrayed in the media was so far removed from where I was that I wondered how I could possibly identify with church people, and how could they possibly identify with me?

Paul was undeterred by my refusals and he was so persistent that eventually I said I would go, but only on one condition: that we go half an hour early. I had reasoned that there wouldn't be anyone there if we went early and so I could slip into the building and hide behind a pillar (I thought every church building had pillars). Then, once the service was over, I could slip out again without being noticed. At least then I could say I'd been and he would stop pestering me.

Paul neglected to tell me that there weren't any pillars in this particular church building and that the people in the church were so passionately in love with Jesus that they would all meet at least an hour before the full service started. When we walked though the door, dozens of people of all ages, backgrounds and nationalities, were already lost in worship. No one greeted me at the door, or even noticed me, because they were all absorbed in praising God.

This was the first time I felt so impacted by the presence of God. I didn't realise that was what it was, but I felt God was reaching deep inside me. There were no words to accurately describe what I was feeling, but it was as though wafting strands of sunlight were streaming inside of me and moving around – like sunlight flowing through the leaves of a tree blowing in the wind.

I felt these strands of warmth both on the inside and outside, like the rays of the sun. It was as though God was speaking deep into the no-man's land of my heart, where deep calls to deep.

He was communicating with me on a level I'd never experienced before.

I felt the tears on my face and I went and sat down right next to the nearest wall, because I was trying to hide as best I could. All I could do was sit on the wooden chair with my forehead pressed against the back of the wooden seat in front of me, trying to bury my face there, as I listened to all these Christians singing their songs of love to Jesus.

Eventually, when the service was over and I could prise my head off the seat in front of me, there was a pool of tears on the floor. I wondered what on earth was happening to me, but I went back again with Paul to the next service, and the same thing happened, and then to the next service, and the next. Every time there would be tears and a sense of God's presence. I knew God was drawing me by his Spirit.

Two weeks later on a Sunday evening, one of the Pentecostal elders of the church was preaching and he made an appeal for salvation. There was such a battle going on inside of me, with part of me wanting to say "yes" but another part of me saying "no" that I didn't respond that night. I felt so bad about it afterwards that I promised God that the next time someone made an appeal, I would definitely respond. I didn't have to wait long. The following Tuesday an Anglican minister called Trevor Dearing and his wife Anne, came to speak at the church.

Trevor had an international ministry of healing and deliverance, and I sat completely absorbed as he told all these amazing God stories. When he came to the end he said,

"Now, before we pray for people to be healed, if there's anyone here who would like to give their life to Jesus, we'd like to invite them to come forward first."

My heart began to pound. "Please God, don't let me be the only one to get up."

The battle inside started up again, but this time I knew I was going to get up and respond. After several minutes had passed I forced myself out of my seat and began to walk towards the front with others who, by then, were going forward for healing.

I went to where Anne was praying and there were about five people in front of me. The man at the front was an elderly gentleman with white hair, and as Anne prayed for him he fell down onto the floor. I began to panic because I thought he'd had a heart attack and someone should call an ambulance, but nobody seemed in the least bit perturbed and the poor guy was just left on the floor.

Then the same thing happened to the second person and then the third. I looked over to where Trevor was praying and people there were also falling down. I'd never come across this before. I certainly didn't like the look of it and I was determined that under no circumstances would I allow it to happen to me!

When the time came for Anne to pray for me, she didn't even ask me what I was there for. Instead she began praying aloud in a foreign language. I couldn't understand a word she was saying, so I just thought, "Well God, I'm here to give my life to you, so that's what I'm going to do."

That night I completely surrendered my life to Jesus Christ and told him I was sorry for the mess my life was in, and that if he could do anything with it then I would give it to him, unreservedly, one hundred per cent. So I gave him my life and asked him to come into my heart. The next thing I knew, I was lying flat on my back on the floor.

While I was lying there I heard God speak to me. It wasn't in an audible voice like human speech, but I knew it was his voice. It came with a sense and an understanding that was almost audible. He said,

"You've been grieving for your father since the age of four and you'll grieve no more."

With that, I felt a huge weight lift off me and eventually, when I got back to my seat, I felt amazing, almost euphoric. That feeling lasted for several months afterwards. I realised that I'd known from the age of four that my father had a problem with drink, and even as a young child my heart had feared for him, and was in fact already grieving. When God spoke to me, he took all that from me. It was so amazing to be free from carrying the weight of all that guilt and responsibility.

That was how my journey with Jesus began and I was floating on air for months afterwards. I never missed a church service and was so hungry to learn and to grow in my new-found faith.

The minister at the Elim Pentecostal church I was going to in Ilford was a man named Barry Killick. He had such a love for the Bible and he took me under his wing and nurtured me on a one-to-one basis. Under his leadership and care I too developed a deep love of the Scriptures.

I was so inquisitive to know more about God that it wasn't unusual for me to read the Bible until two o'clock in the morning, at which point, being unable to force my eyes to stay open any longer, I'd drop off to sleep with the Bible open in front of me on the bed. Then I would wake up in the morning and go straight back to reading where I'd left off the night before.

At the same time I was also taken under the wing of a group of intercessors in the church. They really prayed for me and fed me books on all the great men and women of God of the past.

I learnt so much from these gifted, spiritual people who knew the voice of God. They were all prophetically gifted, but when I'd been a Christian for about a month, one of these intercessors, Grace, said to me,

"God's given me a word for you."

"Great, what is it?" I asked.

"I can't tell you, because God's got to tell you first, and then my word will just confirm what he's already told you."

So I started to pray more earnestly and after another month, I thought I knew what God was saying to me, but I could hardly believe what I was hearing, so I went to Grace and I said,

"Grace, I think God's spoken to me, but I can hardly believe what I think I've heard and I want you to tell me first what it is he's said to you."

"No, you tell me first what it is he's said to you!"

This crazy conversation went backwards and forwards. I argued,

"But if I tell you first, you can just say 'yes, that's it'. How will I know it's God?"

"Because I've got it all written down, it's right here in my handbag."

So I began to tell her that I felt God was saying I would be in full-time ministry; that I'd be doing the things I'm doing now; and when I'd finished, she pulled a piece of paper out of her handbag and gave it to me. On it was written everything that God had spoken to me about and I was left in something of a state of shock.

Those godly women intercessors taught me so much. As I continued to immerse myself in the Scriptures, what really fired me up was reading about what Jesus and his disciples did. I wanted to put into practice what I was reading, so any moment I could, I would pray for people, and when these intercessors, who were my mothers in Christ, became ill, I wouldn't hesitate to go to the hospital to pray for them.

These women were quite elderly, and even though it might have been their time to die, I still prayed my best prayer for their healing. I was devastated whenever God didn't answer those prayers and took them to be with him.

I was so hungry to see people healed and the hunger in my heart was being stirred by the Holy Spirit. Being in God's presence and reading God's word, being around anyone who moved in healing, or going anywhere where I could receive prayer – that was my sole focus.

I could have been so easily put off when nothing happened, but early on I made a conscious decision to believe God's word, even when things around me were speaking to the contrary. Unbelief is a lifestyle choice, just as much as faith is, and I chose to live in faith.

I chose to believe what God said in his word, despite not always seeing what he promised would happen, and somewhere along the way came the revelation that God's reality is greater than this one. So even though I was all too often seeing the effects of this reality and this world, with all my heart I believed that his kingdom was more real than this one.

Reading about Jesus and the disciples doing the things they did really excited me, so I prayed any chance I had, and the more I prayed, the more things began to happen. I began to see signs of God breaking through in healing, but I didn't see anything major happening at this time and much of my experience was quite discouraging.

One night I had a dream in which I saw a woman in a hospital bed with my friend Paul standing beside her, and I saw over her the word "leukaemia". So when I woke up in the morning I phoned Paul and asked him if he knew anyone who was ill at that moment. He said he didn't, but questioned why I was asking him. When I said I'd had a dream, he pressed me to tell him what it was.

A week later I was in his house and the phone rang with the news that one of Paul's friends was in hospital with leukaemia. We were both shocked to hear this, but because of the dream, I went with Paul to the hospital. I began to explain to the woman that the reason I was there was because I'd had this dream in which I felt God was showing me the nature of her illness, and I'd come with Paul because we wanted to pray for her, if that was okay. She agreed and I prayed in tongues and asked God to heal her and we left. Because of the dream, we fully expected her to be healed, so when news of her death came shortly after that visit, we were both shocked and upset.

I believe that was one of the reasons why Paul fell away from God soon after. He couldn't accept that God would give us a word about this situation, only for his friend to die. For myself though, I reasoned that God was sovereign in these things and I didn't know the full story. I didn't know whether she'd maybe accepted Christ at some point, but I was obedient, and I did what I felt God had asked me to do, no more, no less. That was a really hard thing though and Paul went one way and I went the other.

I kept on praying because I knew that there's always hope with Jesus. Yet one of the most distressing and discouraging things for me was praying for sick children whose parents were looking to me as if I was the last hope for their child. The pain I felt when the children weren't visibly healed in front of my eyes and the look of disappointment in the eyes of the parents, nearly made me give up altogether. I actually got to the point where I said to God,

"If I have to pray for any more children where the parents are coming to me and this is their only hope and I'm trying to give them hope in Jesus, I can't bear the pain of that if they're not healed when I pray. And if I have to pray for another child that's not healed, then I don't think I want to pray for another sick child ever again. And not just that, I think I want to quit praying for anybody because it's just too painful."

I was just being honest with God about how I felt. Somehow, I'm not sure how, God dealt with my heart, and what I realised was this: the part that I had to play was to pray my very best prayer and leave the results to God.

3

DOING THE WORK
OF AN EVANGELIST

When I became a Christian, I so wanted to tell everyone about Jesus. When I'd exhausted telling my family and friends, and everyone else I could think of with whom I had even the most tenuous of relationships, I asked our pastor, Barry Killick, whether he had a team that went out onto the streets to tell people about Jesus. At that time the church didn't have such a team, so with his blessing I decided to set about forming one, even though I had no idea how to go about it.

While I was wondering how to tell more people about Jesus, a Jamaican evangelist called George Miller visited our church.

George would visit different churches on missions to preach the gospel and pray for the sick, but it was his practice to take teams with him and work alongside the churches he visited in their on going mission. He travelled round the country, training up teams of Christians from different churches to do evangelism on the streets, and he offered to send someone to our church to train us in street evangelism.

I was convinced that this was the answer to what I'd been asking for, so I went to see Barry to ask him to invite someone from George's team to come to our church. However, a condition was that we had to have first gathered a group of at least five or six people. Barry suggested I recruit a small team, then he invited George to send a couple of his people down and they began to train us in methods like sketch board evangelism and tract evangelism.

It was a moment of divine timing which enabled me to take my first tentative steps outside the walls of the church. My very first venture onto the streets was to do sketch board evangelism and I confess I was absolutely terrified! All the more so because, since it was me who'd put the team together in the first place, Barry was now asking me to lead it. I felt I'd been unwittingly thrust to the fore leading this evangelistic endeavour out onto the streets.

Exactly one year later, I accompanied George to Blackpool on my first mission trip. It was there that for the very first time I saw the power of God move in an amazing way. Deaf ears were opened and we saw deliverances. Even now, all these years later, there are a couple of healings that stand out for me. One was of a lady with a club foot. She was wearing a black boot with a five-inch heel. A young girl, who'd only been a Christian for a couple of months, prayed for her. The lady fell to the floor under the power of the Holy Spirit and while she was lying flat out on the ground, I saw her leg grow out a full five inches, so that the boot was now sticking out unevenly.

When she came to, this young girl said, "I think God has made your leg grow." The woman couldn't believe it. She stood up and was dancing and jumping around at a forty-five-degree angle, joyfully praising God.

The very first person I prayed for on that Blackpool mission trip was a lady who had suffered with epilepsy for over forty years. This was the first time I'd ever prayed for someone and they'd fallen under the power of the Holy Spirit and I wasn't quite sure what to do. She was lying flat out and when she came to and sat up I said,

"I don't think God's finished with you yet," and I prayed again.

Down she went for the second time. That lady was completely healed of her epilepsy and on a return visit to Blackpool a year later, she came to tell me she was completely free of it.

I also experienced God using me in deliverance when I was in Blackpool. I desired to be a blessing to my host and while I was praying about this, God spoke to me about what was stopping him having a closer relationship with God, so when the opportunity came, I offered to pray for him.

God had shown me that, even though he had known it was wrong, my host had sat around a Ouija board and a face had appeared over the board. As I got him to renounce the spirit of the Ouija board he fell to the ground and I heard this strange voice shout out, "I'm not leaving."

From my reading of the Scriptures I knew this was a demon, so I commanded the demon to go and it came out with a blood-curdling shriek. My host was set free. He instantly relaxed, took hold of my hand and said gratefully, "Thank you. The monkey's off my back."

Because the power of God was so evident on our first missions trip there, we returned to Blackpool several times over the following years. Each time we saw God do wonderful things. On only our second trip, during worship at the very beginning of the meeting, the pastor of the church leaned over to speak to George, prompting George to suddenly stand up, raise his hand and call out "Stop!" right in the middle of worship. Everyone was shocked and wondered what on earth was going on. As if interrupting worship was nothing out of the ordinary, George explained,

"The pastor has told me there are some deaf people here who have come to be healed."

I wasn't surprised at the presence of several deaf people, because the previous year we had seen an eight-year-old girl who'd been born deaf, completely healed.

George said, "Where are you? I want to pray for you. Please stand."

Five of them were sitting on the front row, so as to be close enough to lip-read, and they all stood attentively while George prayed for them from the platform, taking authority over the deafness. Wonderfully, all five received their hearing. George smiled and said, "Now you can enjoy the worship and hear what God has to say to you."

You can imagine how that meeting went on from there. God did extraordinary things.

When I was in Blackpool, it was my habit to get up early in the morning and go for a walk along the beach and talk to the Lord. One morning I felt the Lord impress upon me that it was time for me to join George and the ministry of Impact Missions full time.

I said to the Lord that I was willing, but I asked him to speak to George first to confirm it – then I would know it was the right time for me to join Impact Missions. A week later George phoned me up early in the morning to say that God had spoken to him, saying that now was the time for me to come on board, but he added,

"I'm afraid there is no money to pay you Mark. If you accept, you will have to live by faith. Do you need some time to pray about it?"

"George, I was just waiting for your call. God has already spoken to me, and I don't need time to pray about it. It's okay."

So it was that I started working for Impact Missions, leading and overseeing the action teams.

It was only a relatively short time later that I felt God tell me that he was wanting to broaden George's horizons and that he would be moving him on. He clearly indicated to me that when George left, this was my time also to part company with Impact Missions.

God had graciously prepared me for this, so it was no surprise when one day George told me he was leaving, because he believed God was calling him to the West Indies and further afield. George tried to help me feel that he wasn't abandoning me, by saying that he still planned to retain a base in the UK, but he clearly felt he was pulling the rug from under my feet.

I was able to set his mind at ease by telling him that God had already warned me this would be happening, so I could release him freely with my full blessing. I had learnt so much from George, and to this day he has been one of the greatest influences in my life. My heart so resonated with his passion for the lost and his vision to mobilise the Church to reach them. His integrity, faith and the tangible presence of the Holy Spirit that accompanied his ministry has left an indelible mark on my life.

It was at this time that I somehow became an assistant pastor at the Elim church I was saved in. I say "somehow" because I didn't tick any of the boxes. In particular, I had never been ordained.

Nonetheless, Stephen Derbyshire who had by now succeeded Barry Killick as the senior pastor, invited me to join him on the leadership team as an assistant minister with responsibility for evangelism. His invitation coincided with my leaving Impact Missions, so God's timing couldn't have been better.

Yet here I was, heading up evangelism in the Ilford Elim church, all the time thinking how crazy it was. I remember how, as a brand new Christian, I would look at Barry Killick on the platform, thinking what an amazing preacher he was, and thinking that I'd never be able to even stand up there, let alone preach like that. So to suddenly find myself on the same platform doing just that, left me wondering how on earth I'd ever got there.

Wynne Lewis, the general superintendent of the Elim Church kept asking me whether I'd done my exams, and although I felt guilty about not having done them, I never was motivated to complete them – probably because I found myself fully occupied with taking missions teams here there and everywhere.

Accompanying me on many of these trips was a lovely young girl from Essex. She was passionate about Jesus and shared my heart for reaching the lost, and although I'd never thought of marriage previously, I realised that God was drawing us together. Linda and I were married in the summer of 1989, just after we'd finished the Billy Graham mission to West Ham.

Thereafter, Linda travelled with me whenever her work allowed, and wherever I went I would teach and train the church in the same evangelistic methods I'd been taught and trained in when I was with George. We'd go out onto the streets with the sketch board and then invite the people we'd contacted in our outreach to come along to a healing meeting in the church we were working with.

My heart was always to see the signs and wonders that were happening in church meetings happening on the streets. One of my frustrations, when I'd visit places, was that in the church meetings, although the people would be tremendously blessed, the ones coming along were, for the most part, already Christians. My passion was to reach those on the outside, not those who were already part of the church.

I had another frustration. We had to invite people to come to healing meetings in the church building because we couldn't get the church out to do that on the streets. We would have a wonderful time in the church meetings, but I knew the ministry wouldn't continue after I'd left, because the Christians weren't equipped to follow me out onto the streets. To do what I'd been taught to do in church on the streets was something completely different.

Ephesians 4:11-12 says,

"It was he who gave some to be apostles, some to be prophets, some to be evangelists, and some to be pastors and teachers, to prepare God's people for works of service, so that the body of Christ may be built up."

From my reading of these verses I could see that God had given to the church people especially gifted in certain areas, who were called not only to operate in their particular gifting but to equip the church for works of service.

I could see that with my own God-given gifts of healing and evangelism, I could go to a church community where not much healing and evangelism was taking place and, because of my gifting, I would see more happen than most, and have faith to press in for a breakthrough.

I knew that God was using me as a catalyst to release healing and salvation, but I wanted that to continue after I left, and the only way for that to happen was to somehow find a way to equip the church to minister on the streets. This was my dilemma. How could I find a way to take the mystery out of it for people? How could I find a way to take the church by the hand and show them how to do what I did?

I could teach people the things I'd been taught to do, but I had no model for teaching them the things that I'd done simply out of obedience to God, because no one had taught me to do that. I longed to find a safe way for the church to leave the security of its own walls and move back out into the marketplace where I felt it belonged.

4

GO, HEAL THE SICK

❧

Working with Impact Missions I'd been trained in doing things like sketch board evangelism, street preaching, using questionnaires, mime, drama, tract evangelism and door-to-door work – all kinds of different evangelistic methods – but God now began to move me away from that.

I had taken a team to Sandwell in Dudley and we were stationed in a pedestrianized area outside a shopping centre. It was a spot where any evangelist's heart would beat faster because thousands of people were walking past. Seeing crowds of people always stirs me, because if God chooses to break through in such a busy place, there is the potential for many to be swept into the kingdom at one time.

We began our outreach there with this drama sketch called "The chicken sketch" which is forever seared on my memory. Part of the sketch involved running around pretending to be a chicken. Thirty grown-up men and women, along with me, were running around the street in circles flapping our arms and clucking like chickens.

I'd prayed beforehand, "Lord, if this is the way to connect the brokenness of our streets with the love of your heart, then I'm going to be the best chicken there could ever be."

But as people were going by you could see the look of embarrassment on their faces, almost as if they were saying to everyone, "Please don't look at them, whatever you do, the poor demented things. Don't make it any worse for them than it already is."

And in that moment, I felt how ridiculous we all looked. Small wonder the people weren't paying the blindest bit of attention to us. In fact they were purposefully ignoring us, because they were embarrassed for us.

After that I thought,

"God, there's got to be a better way than this."

I'd been reading in the Bible how Jesus went around performing miracles, signs and wonders, and I was gripped by reading about how Philip the evangelist proclaimed Christ and how, in Acts 8:6, "When the crowds heard Philip and saw the miraculous signs he did, they all paid close attention to what he said."

It was at that point that I knew I couldn't go on being a chicken any longer! I needed to take a walk to talk with the Lord. As I did, I was so focussed on my one-way conversation with the Lord, pouring out my complaint to him, that it was a surprise when I suddenly came to the end of the town and face to face with a large bronze sculpture of a huge fist grasping a cross. The image of the cross and the size of the sculpture was arresting.

I had come to the very spot where John Wesley had arrived on horseback to preach to the multitudes in the mid 1700s. The bronze commemorated Wesley's visit to the town and had been erected on some stone steps to represent the horse-mounting block which Wesley stood on, so that all the people could see and hear him as he preached.

I recalled how the glory of God fell when Wesley preached and as I pictured him preaching in this very place, I began to thank God for everything that he'd done when Wesley was ministering on the streets, and to pray that God's glory would once again fall on these very same streets.

In that moment I heard the Lord say, "Go, heal the sick."

I turned round and went back to the rest of the team with renewed hope and inspiration. I knew I had heard the Lord's voice, but I didn't know how I was going to set about following his instructions. I still didn't have any plan formulated in my mind by the time I got back, but I tore a sheet off the sketch board pad and wrote up in big letters, "Healing and Miracles Here. Jesus Heals". Then I took the microphone and began to invite people to come forward for prayer if they needed healing.

The first person to come forward was a man who wanted to give up smoking. He said he'd been to the doctors and had tried everything, all to no avail. As nothing else had worked, he was willing to try prayer. I led him in a prayer renouncing the addiction and then I prayed for him. While there was no visible sign of anything happening while I prayed, when I'd finished the man took a packet of cigarettes from his coat pocket, crumpled them in his hand and dropped them at my feet.

When I looked down and saw that crushed packet of cigarettes on the ground, I took the microphone with renewed vigour and boldness and proclaimed loudly and confidently,

"If anyone wants to quit smoking, you can be set free now. God wants to set you free."

A huge queue began to form and the packets of cigarettes began piling up. As they did so, a passer-by went to pick them up, but I said, "Leave them alone, they're mine." Those cigarettes were my trophy and no one was going to take them from me.

Someone then came and asked, "Well, I suffer from arthritis. Can God heal me of this condition?"

From then on, I resolved in my heart that whenever I was out on the streets, I was going to pray for the sick, because Jesus had said, "Go, heal the sick and tell the people the kingdom of God is near." It was so simple, I wondered how I'd missed it all this time.

Thereafter, every time I went onto the streets, God broke through in signs and wonders and it was an amazing thing. Prayer for healing often ended up with people falling flat on their backs on the concrete pavements. It wasn't unusual to see streets full of bodies as members of the public were laid out under the power of God.

On one occasion I was in Weston super Mare and it had been raining. The cobbled high street was on an incline and pools of rainwater had collected in the cobblestones. When I began to pray for the sick, an elderly lady came up for prayer. She was wearing a raincoat and had a pleated plastic rain bonnet tied under her chin and a handbag over her right shoulder. I shot up an arrow prayer, "Lord, please don't let her fall on the ground because she's in her eighties and I don't want her to get soaked. But Lord, we need a sign and a wonder here."

I asked her, "What would you like Jesus to do for you?"

She told me she had arthritis in the back of her neck, so I placed my hand on the back of her neck and commanded the arthritis to go. All of a sudden she flopped forward touching her toes. It was as though her legs were fixed in cement, but from the waist up she was out in the Spirit. My right hand was on the back of her neck still and as I saw her handbag fall off her right shoulder I went to catch it with my left hand.

The pastor of the church we were ministering with came over to me with a look of horror on his face, wondering what on earth I was doing to the poor woman. By now a crowd had gathered and everyone was staring at me with my right hand still on the back of her neck and my left hand holding her handbag as the woman was touching her toes.

I quickly took my hand away and she remained touching her toes while I preached for twenty minutes. I wasn't quite sure what to do. I was always surprised by what God did, but I was worried about the poor lady's back, so I touched her on the forehead and she stood upright and turned her neck from side to side. She was completely healed. No arthritis.

Those kind of things were often happening.

Wherever I went, I taught people to do what I'd been taught to do by George Miller and Impact Missions – how to make an appeal for salvation, how to lay hands on the sick and pray for people – but it was still in the context of a church healing meeting. I hadn't yet worked out a way to equip the church to minister on the streets. But God was opening many doors for me both in the UK and further afield; his manifest presence on the streets was increasing and one thing always seemed to lead on to another. In a roundabout way, this was how I came to go to Pakistan.

I took a team to encourage a church in Edmonton Green and teach them some evangelism. The church had been reaching out into the community and they were especially trying to connect with the people living in a high-rise block of flats there. So I visited them over a weekend and began to teach them sketch board and tract evangelism. I knew God had so much more though, so after we'd done the sketch board, I tore off a sheet of paper and wrote "Miracles and Healing" on it.

I saw a woman who God gave me a word of knowledge for because he wanted to set her free. She agreed to have some prayer and so she came and stood in front of me. By this time I always made sure that someone was standing behind the person being prayed for to catch them, so they wouldn't fall on the ground. As I began to pray for this lady, a mother and a daughter walked by. Both were Greek and the mother turned to the daughter and said in Greek,

"That man is trying to fool everyone into believing that Jesus heals today. He died 2,000 years ago. That's the end of the story."

But standing next to me was one of the leaders of the church, whose name was John. It just so happened that John was Greek, so he'd understood what the mother had said and he stopped them in their tracks when he replied back to them in their native tongue,

"Why don't you believe that Jesus Christ is the same yesterday, today and for ever? Just watch what he's going to do."

I love leaders who are full of faith and John's response galvanised my prayer. To my surprise, as I prayed for this woman, she dived face forward past me, spun around in mid air and somehow landed behind me on her back. It was an astonishing manoeuvre on her part and I looked at the bemused person standing behind her, gesturing "Why didn't you catch her?"

The effect of this was to draw a big crowd and all afternoon people were getting healed and set free. Every single one testified over the microphone to what God had done for them. And the mother and daughter who stood and watched both gave their hearts to Jesus at the end. It truly was the most extraordinary day.

Some two or three months later, I was in my flat and a blue airmail letter came through the letterbox. I opened it up to discover that it was from a pastor in Pakistan who was pleading with me to come to his village in the north of the country.

Since I didn't know any pastors in Pakistan, I thought the letter was a scam. I put it to one side, having no intention of responding to it, let alone going to Pakistan. But about an hour later the telephone rang and a man with a Pakistani accent said,

"Mark, you don't know me, but I was at Edmonton Green a few months ago and I saw God doing signs and wonders through you on the streets. I spoke to the pastor of the church in Pakistan that I grew up in and I told him about you and what I witnessed. Have you, by any chance, received a letter from him?"

Somewhat surprised I replied,

"Yes, as a matter of fact, a letter arrived in the post this morning."

"Well, in there is a genuine invitation to go to Pakistan. Would you please prayerfully consider going?"

I didn't really want to go to Pakistan, so I began to pray like this,

"Lord, if you really, really want me to go to Pakistan you will have to make it really, really clear, because I really, really don't want to go!"

That Sunday as I went to church as usual, a lady whose sister had recently died and gone to be with Jesus, greeted me at the door with these words:

"Mark, I had a dream about you last night. In my dream, I saw my sister standing on a street corner and she was handing tracts out to passers by. When she saw me she came over and gave me a great big hug and asked me, 'Can you go to Pakistan?'

'When I said no, she asked,

'Is there anyone in your church you can send?' and I said,

'Yes, Mark can go.'

'Well send him, because God is blessing the work in Pakistan and if Mark goes, God will bless Mark.'"

When she'd finished relating the dream to me, she said,

"Does that mean anything to you?"

"Maybe" was all I replied.

In the meantime I thought it might be prudent to ask a few like-minded people to pray about how they might feel about coming with me to Pakistan – should I happen to go.

Then I had a phone call from one of the elders of the church whose name was Lector. Lector was from Jamaica. He had a very deep voice and was extremely good at spinning a yarn. He said to me,

"Mark, I'm in the church building and you'll never guess who's standing next to me."

"Who?"

"It's the Bishop of Pakistan and he wants to speak to you."

"The Bishop of Pakistan is standing next to you, in our church building, and he wants to speak to me? Put him on the line!"

I thought he was pulling my leg.

At first there was silence, then this heavily accented voice said,

"Hallo. My name is Samuel and I'm the Bishop of Pakistan."

"Lector that's the best impersonation I've ever heard you do!"

"No, no! I really am the Bishop of Pakistan!"

Then this man began to explain how he'd been on a preaching tour of America before he'd hopped on a plane to the UK to visit his very best friend who he'd been at school with. It just so happened that his best friend was a member of our church.

This was when I began to panic. Samuel went on,

"My friend informs me that you are thinking of going to Pakistan. Well, we have a small gathering every year of about 50,000 people and I would like to give you a personal invitation to come and minister to us."

I held up my hands in surrender.

"Yes, Lord, I'll go."

In September of 1994 I went to that nation and saw God do wonderful things. It was such an encouragement to the church there. Despite my initial reluctance to go, and the difficulties of ministering there, it turned out to be one of the best trips I have ever taken.

We peer into the mist and see a little of so much more. Fear settles for the little. Faith steps into the more.

Some events in our lives might seem completely random, but I have come to appreciate that in God's design for each of our lives, every place we go and every person we meet is important and significant. When we are willing to cooperate with God, little by little he unfolds a plan for our life that brings him glory and makes our life one great adventure of faith.

As long as the Holy Spirit navigates, the route we take is unimportant.

5

THE CHINESE CHURCH

While I was in the Ilford Elim church, God had spoken to me about working amongst the Chinese. At the time I thought that meant I would be going to Hong Kong, because Phyllis White, who was one of the intercessors in the church, had given me a book about Jackie Pullinger, Chasing the Dragon. Phyllis, who was always feeding me books about great men and women of God and the work of the Holy Spirit, was a good friend of Jackie's, and she'd been writing to Jackie about me and what I was doing in the church. She told me that there was a place for me at St Stephen's Society[1], and all that was needed was for me to say "Yes".

Jackie Pullinger was seeing heroin addicts set free in a matter of days with no cold turkey, just prayer, and I got really excited because this seemed like the most wonderful tailor-made opportunity for me. So I put this before God, as I did with every decision in my life, and to my surprise, felt a definite "No" from the Lord. It was really hard for me to tell Phyllis that I wouldn't be going to Hong Kong after all.

It was also somewhat confusing for me because I knew that the Lord had spoken to me about working amongst the Chinese. I didn't understand why he didn't want me to go and work with Jackie. I kept hearing about everything God was doing through her ministry and my heart was always to be where God was moving and where miracles were taking place. I then began to wonder whether I was supposed to go to China instead, but because God had said "No" to Hong Kong and was silent on my questions about China, I decided to stop second-guessing God and put the whole thing on the back burner.

Some time later, I was preaching in an evening meeting at an Assemblies of God church in Kent, and when we offered to pray for people at the end of the meeting, a Chinese woman came up for prayer. God really touched her and when he did, he reminded me, "You will be ministering amongst the Chinese."

After I'd prayed for her, the pastor of the church, Doug Bean, came up to me and said,

"Do you see that Chinese lady you prayed for there? Well, she used to come to this church but she's now going to a Chinese church in London, where she has an evangelistic ministry. I don't know why she came along here tonight, but just as you were praying for her, I felt God say to me that you are to go and help this church."

Immediately I felt this was God's confirmation to me that I was to go and help this group of Chinese believers. In the unique way God has of connecting people with his purposes, through Doug I was introduced to this Chinese woman, and she in turn was instrumental in introducing me to the Salvation for Chinese Church in London.

I went along to encourage the congregation and teach them some street evangelism. While I was doing some training weekends with them in London, one of this lady's three brothers came to me and said,

"Mark, my brothers and sister and I have been Christians for a while now, but we've always felt that something's kept us from getting closer to God. Last night I dreamt that we were offered up to idols as babies and that each of us was named after an idol. We brothers have changed our names now, to Aaron, John and Joshua, but our sister hasn't changed her name. She is still named after one of these idols. Could you please pray for us? We think this is what has been hindering us from getting closer to God."

In front of the whole congregation I led the family in a prayer renouncing all of these idols by name. When I turned to the sister, however, she began to physically attack me and her brothers had to jump on her to restrain her. The rest of the church were in a state of shock because they'd never seen deliverance before and they all heard the demon say that it could not leave this woman, because if it did, many Chinese would no longer believe in the idol and would turn to Christ.

"Great!" I said, "Get out!"

The demon left the woman with a shriek and some commotion ensued. There was a lot of panic among the other leaders because many of the church congregation had been offered up to idols at some point and they were worried about what would now happen to them. But I didn't want to be distracted from the training I was doing, or diverted from my goal of getting this church out onto the streets of London. I reasoned that we could deal with deliverance another time, but right now we were all going to go out onto Gerrard Street in Chinatown. This calmed the situation down and we had an amazing time. What made it so special was that this dear Chinese lady who had been delivered led someone to Jesus.

My relationship with the Chinese church was growing and about this time there was an English-speaking Chinese congregation called Emmanuel Evangelical Church (EEC) that had just begun to experience a move of the Holy Spirit. It was something that was relatively new to them and they were keen to learn and experience more.

The year was 1994 and there was a powerful move of the Holy Spirit in Canada, which came to be known around the world as the "Toronto Blessing". There was a lot of controversy surrounding what was happening there, but being hungry to discover more about the Holy Spirit, this English-speaking group of Chinese believers decided to travel there to see what was happening for themselves.

Their visit to Toronto left them more desirous than ever for the Holy Spirit and his gifts, so on their return, the Singaporean pastor of EEC, Chua Wee-Hian, approached the Salvation for Chinese Church to ask if they knew anyone who could help them with this move of the Holy Spirit.

So it was that we were introduced to one another and I was invited to go and speak at EEC one bitterly cold Sunday morning in February.

By this time I was seeing signs and wonders happening wherever I went, so on this particular morning I was sharing several stories with the congregation about God breaking out on the streets. When I'd finished Wee-Hian came up to the microphone and said,

"Now we're going to follow Mark out onto Oxford Street to put into practice everything he's been telling us."

This was news to me. I thought I must have missed something, but what I hadn't fully appreciated was that Wee-Hian wanted to make sure that I was the real deal if he was going to invite me to come and help them.

So we went out onto Oxford Street after the service on that freezing cold morning. The whole church of around a hundred and fifty people followed me out. One musician brought a guitar, but he was only able to play one worship song because his fingers were too numb with the cold. Then all eyes turned to me.

I stood there with no props at all and I began to preach. Then I invited people to come for prayer. A South American man came forward who couldn't speak a word of English, but his friend translated for him and I learnt that he'd recently had an operation which was unsuccessful and he was in a lot of pain. I asked him if he had any beliefs or religious background, but he was totally un-churched.

Sleet was now beginning to fall and the man kept his eyes unblinkingly fixed on me as I laid my hand on his head and took authority over the injury and commanded it to be healed. Suddenly his eyes looked as if they were about to pop out on stalks as he stared at me and started to fall face down to the ground.

When he was at about a forty-five degree angle to the ground I managed to grab hold of him and physically turn him around to stop his face hitting the concrete and lay him on his back. His eyes were still wide open as the sleet was settling on him, and I preached now to a gathering crowd. Eventually the man got up off the ground, a big smile on his face, and his friend and translator said he had been completely healed.

It was so cold that morning that I'm amazed anything happened, but the church just needed something they could see with their own eyes. With that Wee-Hian invited me to a meeting with him later in the week and he asked if I could help them. I knew now that this was what God wanted me to do, because he'd already used me to help the other Chinese church, so at the end of March 1996 I went to work with Wee-Hian.

By now Wee-Hian's church had grown to the point where they had to find a new place to meet, so he and I scoured the area looking at different buildings, but they were all too small for what we believed God wanted to do. Eventually though, this property came up in Marsham Street close to the Houses of Parliament and Westminster Abbey. We made an appointment to view it and when we walked into the foyer of what is now Emmanuel Centre, we knew at once that this was the place God had for us.

We made a bid for this property at a starting price of £1,000,000 and eventually bought it for £1,250,000. When we were given the keys, the very next day we were offered £8,000,000 for the freehold! God provided for that building in an amazing way, but that is another story.

We held our first service there on 25 May 1997 and within eight months of our being in that building, over 60,000 people had come through the doors. Because we felt we were stewards of the property, we had different streams coming in and using the building. The Pioneer church held weekly revival meetings at Marsham Street from June 1997 to April 1999, and different people and ministries were coming from all over the world to pray, worship, and hold conferences there.

It was such an exciting time to be part of all that God was doing at Emmanuel Centre, but it was also the time God chose to speak to me about moving to Northern Ireland.

1. Jackie Pullinger founded St Stephen's Society in 1981 to provide rehabilitation homes for recovering drug addicts, prostitutes and gang members.

6

CALLED TO NORTHERN IRELAND

Over the course of the years I'd been to Northern Ireland on several occasions and travelled all around the north and south of the country on missions. My first visit was during "The Troubles". I recalled the ambushes and roadblocks and what a shock it was to see weapons visibly carried on the streets. People thought I was crazy going there, especially going and preaching on the Shankhill road in Belfast! Of all the places I didn't want to live, and where I certainly didn't want to raise three young boys, Northern Ireland was probably top of the list.

Yet on the other hand, on my first visit to Coleraine I'd witnessed some of the most amazing healings I'd ever experienced out on the streets. And as I now began to seriously pray and consider this move, the memories of that first visit came flooding back.

Two weeks before I'd been due to go there, I had been sitting in my father-in-law's house. To while the time away, I'd picked up his Daily Telegraph newspaper and randomly opened it up to where there was a news column with the heading "Shoppers' Exodus".

I began to read about the shopkeepers in Coleraine who were complaining about street evangelists, saying that because of their vehement and uncompromising message of "turn or burn", they were driving shoppers away from the town centre, because the people were fed up of hearing this message. They were proposing that all street evangelists be banned from the streets of Coleraine because they were losing so much business.

I could hardly believe what I was reading. In a fortnight's time I was going to hold a mission in a place where people were already hardened to the gospel!

On that first visit we were given permission to hold a healing meeting after The Lord Mayor's parade had finished. It seemed like a great opportunity because the streets were already thronging with people who'd come to see the floats and we were permitted to start our meeting as soon as the barriers along the roadside were removed.

We asked the police what time the last float was due to pass and advertised the timing of our meeting accordingly. The last float went by fifteen minutes before we were expecting it to, and to keep the people's attention, one of our team, Robbie Jay, who was a contemporary gospel singer and saxophonist from Atlanta, sang and played while the council workers were removing the barriers.

Because of what I'd read in the Daily Telegraph, and believing the people to be hardened to the gospel, I decided to emphasise God's love, so when Robbie had finished I took the microphone and spoke for a few brief minutes so as not to lose any of the crowds. I told the people that God loved them and invited them to come forward if they needed healing. Nobody moved.

All the barriers had gone now, but the people hadn't moved,

so I spoke for another ten minutes and made the appeal for healing again. The people remained as unresponsive as before, so I spoke for a further ten minutes, making the same appeal again. Again, there was no response. This continued for a whole hour.

I was completely stumped. I didn't know why the people were neither coming forward nor moving away. Finally, I asked the Lord, "What's holding the people back from responding?" and had the distinct impression that it was fear and pride.

So I prayed publicly over the hundreds of people standing there watching. I closed my eyes because I was afraid they would all walk away when I began to pray, and I took authority over fear and pride and then began to release the presence of God and the love of God over the people of Coleraine. When I opened my eyes, I was surprised to see that all the people were still rooted to the spot, but this time when I asked people to respond if they needed God's touch on their lives, a man stepped forward and said,

"I've been trying to quit smoking for years. I've tried doctors and hypnotherapists, but nothing's worked."

I'd seen many people set free from cigarette addiction, so I said, "Jesus can set you free."

I led him in a prayer renouncing the addiction to nicotine, the craving and the smoking and commanded the addiction to leave, and the man instantly fell to the ground. The crowd that had been stationary all that time took one step forward as I began to explain to them what God was doing.

I then made another appeal and another person stepped forward. This time it was a woman who'd had an operation and was in pain. She fell to the ground and then got up completely healed.

The third person to respond to the appeal for healing was a student from Belfast who had double vision and couldn't see without her glasses. I asked her to remove her glasses and handed them to Robbie Jay as I laid my hands over her eyes, took authority over the blindness and commanded it to leave. She also fell to the ground and when she got up, she was amazed because she could see perfectly. The two friends with her were hugging her and chattering excitedly. Robbie handed her glasses back, but she just laughed and said, "I don't need them now, I'm healed."

The next person to receive prayer was a man in his 60s. He also fell to the ground under the power of God and for a full twenty minutes he remained completely motionless. His wife went over to one of the team and expressed her concern because her husband had recently had a heart bypass operation and he hadn't moved. The team member replied,

"Don't worry, God's doing his own operation, but we'll pick him up off the ground."

They lifted him up, but he was still completely out under the power of God. They propped him up against a wall and it was another ten minutes before he came round with the biggest grin ever on his face. After that people began to push forward to receive healing and one after another publicly testified to being healed. Eventually the crowd were packed in so tight that people were climbing trees to see what God was doing.

A woman had brought her mother for healing. She was paralysed from the waist down and was in a wheelchair. A lady far back in the crowd asked one of the team, "Do you really think God could heal this woman?" because she was thinking to herself, "If I see God heal this woman, I'm going to go and get my aunt who's also paralysed and in a wheelchair."

The team member said, "Yes, I believe Jesus can heal this woman."

I laid my hands gently on this lady's head. People were pressing in so close to see that there was no room. I didn't feel anything in particular as I prayed my best prayer for this woman, but what stood out for me in that moment was the presence of God in that place. The atmosphere was impregnated with a holy awe and reverence. It was the atmosphere of heaven. It was electrifying and everyone could feel God's presence.

After I'd finished praying a very short prayer, I said, "Do something with your legs you've not been able to do before."

The woman's legs began to kick out and, on seeing this, her daughter burst into tears, knowing her mother had been healed.

"Would you like to go for a walk?" I asked.

"Oh yes!"

Some people tried to help her out of the wheelchair, but because I wanted all the glory to go to God, I said, "Please leave her alone. The God who heals her legs will give her strength in her body to stand up and walk." And he did.

She got out of the wheelchair and walked. The crowd erupted in praise and worship. They were clapping, shouting, whistling and many people were weeping. As the crowd parted to let her walk, the woman who had asked the question "Do you really think God could heal this woman?" was heard saying, "This is amazing!" Then when the woman turned round to walk back and she was finally able to get a clear view of her, she immediately recognised her and shouted out, "That's my aunt!" and burst into tears.

Many people pressed forward for prayer after that, but the

crowd was so thick that many weren't able to get close. There was a gospel bus parked by the Town Hall and the workers there reported groups of people going to the bus and saying, "We've seen miracles today and we want to know, how do we become Christians?"

A man called Jerry was in Coleraine that day and seeing the crowds of people, came over to find out what was going on. He was a Christian, but had grown disillusioned with his faith and was no longer following Jesus. I was praying at the time for a man with a built-up shoe who had one leg shorter than the other. As Jerry saw the leg grow out, it turned his life around. He reconnected with Jesus and for the next ten to fifteen years God gave him a prophetic ministry in his job that also turned around the lives of others who had grown disillusioned and had resorted to alcohol.

As I reflected on that first visit to Coleraine in 1992, I realised just how incredibly significant it was. It was only a few months later that the IRA bombed the town and it was severely damaged.

I also remembered some prophetic words I'd been given about God calling me to Northern Ireland and I really felt that God was speaking to me now about moving there.

People often ask me how I hear the voice of God and the only way I can describe it is like a strong impression, akin to the returning echo of a drop of water falling into a deep well. If you miss that returning echo, or if you're not listening out for it, then you're going to miss his voice.

A combination of things were coming together to clarify for me that this was the Lord, so I now went to the church leaders at EEC and told them I believed God was calling me to go to Northern Ireland. They suggested we all pray and fast for three weeks first, to see what God would say to us.

As things turned out, in the very last week before the leaders were going to come together to see what God had been saying, Cindy Jacobs, a gifted prophetic intercessor, came to do some seminars and teaching at the church. I purposely avoided her because I had a feeling that God was going to speak through her!

It was the habit of the church leaders to meet at 8am every Sunday morning to pray for an hour and then to pray for another hour after that with the intercessors. On the morning Cindy was due to speak to the church, the leaders came together to pray and Wee-Hian went round to every one asking what God had said about me moving to Ireland, and not one of them had heard anything. I felt for them, because I knew that in their hearts, they didn't want me to go.

I still really wanted to be certain that this was God speaking, however, because I didn't want to make such a major move without being sure.

Cindy Jacob's visit reinforced the call. After preaching she announced that she was going to prophesy, and I decided to go and stand behind the people she was prophesying over, to catch them in case they fell. I'm greedy for whatever God has. If it's available I want it, so I was listening to Cindy prophesying over this man in a business suit, all the while saying to myself,

"Yes, I receive that Lord ... and yes, I'll have that too."

Cindy suddenly stopped and bent to one side to look behind the businessman. When she saw me there, she said, "Excuse me, could you please step back. You're receiving everything that's for this man here."

When she finished prophesying for him and I turned to sit down, she took me by the wrist and gave me her full attention.

At that point I knew she was going to prophesy for me, so I prayed,

"Now Lord, if this is wrong, tell everybody. Make it abundantly clear, because I don't want to make a mistake. But if this is right, then let the church know so they can release me with their blessing."

What she began to prophesy for me was all the places around the world where God was going to move in signs and wonders, and she reeled off a whole load of countries where she saw stadiums filled with people and many coming to know Jesus. She went on to say that God had opened a door for me and I had to go through it.

I knew then that God had spoken to the church and after that the leaders released me with their blessing to go.

7

COMING TO COLERAINE

As with any major relocation, there are a lot of practical issues that need to be sorted. The house in London was on the market, but it wasn't selling, so we had to make the decision as to whether our move would be dependent on the sale of our house. Linda and I decided that whether we sold or not, we were definitely going. We fixed the date for our departure and, incredibly, found a buyer the very day before we left, so God's timing was perfect.

We moved over to Northern Ireland with our three young sons, Joshua, Timothy and Jordan, on 21 August 1998, and settled in Coleraine.

God had told me that I was to lay my public ministry down, so I had to find some means of earning a living. Suitable employment was in short supply, but I decided to apply for a job with a double-glazing firm. First, however, I wanted to be sure that I could sell their doors and windows without compromising my Christian values. When I went for the interview this was uppermost in my mind. So I asked the interviewer,

"Can I do this job and keep a clear conscience? Can I sell these windows and sleep at night?"

The poor interviewer spent the next hour selling the company to me! He so convinced me about the quality of the product that I took the job.

When I started working we had three weeks of intensive training, after which I knew my windows inside out. My attitude was that I was selling windows for God and I wanted to be the best window salesman ever. Colossians 3:23 says, "Whatever you do, work at it with all your heart, as working for the Lord, not for men." And that was what I was determined to do.

During training, the other salesmen would ask me what I used to do before, so I'd say I'd been working as an evangelist. This was met with stony silence. No one knew what an evangelist was or did. If anyone dared to ask "What's an evangelist?" I just repeated something that I once heard from a wise man,

"Well it's just one beggar telling another where to find bread."

"Oh. Right."

I felt I'd be working there a long time, so I wasn't in a hurry to lay all my cards on the table. It was enough that my employers knew that I followed Jesus.

I didn't have a base salary, I was employed on a commission-only basis, so the bottom line was that if I didn't sell any windows I wasn't going to make any money. Over the four-year period I was there, I saw many people come and go, but I felt this was where I could trust God. I knew I could prove God faithful to provide and was confident I'd get work.

One of the ways this happened was through my blissful ignorance of the religious and political situation in Northern Ireland. Although I asked people, no one seemed able to tell me what all "The Troubles" were about. So when there were jobs going in areas where the other salesmen wouldn't go, the company sent me, and as I was none the wiser. I gladly and willingly went wherever they sent me and all people would say to me was,

"So, you're not from these parts are you?"

I respected people everywhere I went and I never had any trouble. I just saw myself releasing God's goodness and the people I visited responded in kind.

In the beginning I wondered how to behave when there was a conflict between doing my job of selling windows and ministering as a Christian. At the same time, I didn't want to use my being a Christian as a means of selling windows. "Oh, by the way, I'm a Christian, you can trust me not to tell you any lies." If customers bought the windows, I wanted them to do it on the basis of how I presented them, and if it hadn't been a product I actually believed in, I could never have sold it.

I was also in a bit of a dilemma over what I should do if I went into a house where clearly there was someone who was sick. My initial reaction would be to ask them if I could pray for them. But God told me he was going to lead me, so I reasoned that I was going to just follow him in everything, and that if he didn't prompt me or show me, I wouldn't do a thing.

My car boot was loaded up with these smart bags of extremely heavy window samples, complete with glass, locks and steel reinforcing. On one of my very first jobs I was lugging them into the living room of this house when I saw a man sitting in an armchair. His foot was heavily bandaged and a pair of crutches lay beside the armchair.

He apologised to me that he wasn't able to help me in with the bags and began to explain how he'd injured himself. He'd been unhooking a trailer from a vehicle when the towing coupling slipped through his hands and crushed his foot. Now he couldn't put any weight on it.

I wanted to give him the best window demonstration he had ever had. So I began my presentation, even though all the time it was apparent this couple were not in a position to buy. When I was packing away, he said to me,

"You've done me so much good today."

"How's that?" I asked.

"You've made my foot better."

My mind was racing, trying to figure out a logical explanation for this. I thought maybe he'd seen me in Coleraine when I was praying for the sick, while I was working with Impact Missions, and he'd put two and two together and was expecting his foot to be healed.

"Ah, so you've seen me before in Coleraine. You know what I used to do."

"No, I've never seen you before tonight, but as you were demonstrating a window, well, I felt heat go through my leg and into my foot and look..."

He stood up and stamped his foot and his wife was shouting, "Sit down. Sit down."

To my astonishment, the man was completely healed, without my uttering a single word of prayer! I then had the privilege of leading both him and his wife to Jesus.

When I left that house my head was in a daze and I realised that even by my just being there, healing was being released.

God also showed me another way to minister in people's homes. Many couples would offer me a cup of coffee and say to me,

"You're not from around here, are you?"

"No, I lived in London before I came to live here," I would say, to which they would invariably reply,

"What brought you over here?"

"That's a really good question," I would say. "Let's finish business, then afterwards I'll have that cup of coffee you promised and we'll have a chat."

Once my bags were put away, I began to tell them the story of how God had called me to share his love with the people of Northern Ireland and in that way, whether they bought windows or not, I got to lead people to Jesus and pray with them.

God also gave me some wonderful opportunities to minister to my work colleagues and to be a blessing to the company I worked for.

On one occasion I'd noticed that Colin, one of my work colleagues, had been hobbling around in obvious pain for a couple of days. I didn't want to appear nosy, but his discomfort was so obvious that eventually I asked him what was wrong.

"Well, it's like this," he explained. "I was a keen motorbiker, but some years ago I had an accident and came off my bike. I badly injured my knees and broke one of my legs and now, whenever it rains or it's damp, I get this really painful arthritis in my knees."

I said to him, "You know I'm a Christian and I follow Jesus. I have seen people healed and believe God heals today. Could I please pray for you that God would heal you?"

"Well, okay then," he shrugged.

"It's time for our lunch break. Shall we go into the back room where there's a bit of privacy?"

We got up to go when Liam, who was the branch manager,

overheard me and asked, "Can I come as well?"

"Sure," I smiled.

So Liam, Colin and I went into the back room where the training seminars were held and Liam perched on the edge of the table, while Colin sat on a chair and said,

"Before you pray for me, I need to tell you a few things about what's going on here. When I broke my leg, it set so that one leg is now actually shorter than the other and it's putting a lot of pressure on my knees."

My ears pricked up at that because I had a lot of faith for legs to grow.

"And the other thing I've got which is really painful..." and he pulled up his trouser leg to reveal this hugely swollen sac of fluid that had collected below his kneecap. It looked incredibly painful. I'd never seen anything like it before and Liam gasped when he saw it. Colin went on,

"I have to have this syringed when it gets to this point and it's extremely sore."

He was clearly in dreadful pain and I didn't want to waste any time, so I said, "Okay, let me pray for you. Liam, have you ever seen a leg grow? Watch this and see what God's going to do."

I held Colin's legs out and prayed and as his leg began to grow out he said in astonishment,

"The pain's going, the pain's going!" Then a moment later, "The pain's gone!"

Liam nearly fell off the table in shock at what he was seeing, while Colin stood up and started to walk round, completely elated that he'd been healed. The water on his knee however, was still there, so to encourage him further, I advised him,

"Colin, I believe God is in the process of healing you."

The next day when I came into the office, Liam was so excited.

"Mark, have you heard the news?" he asked.

"No, what's happened?"

"It's Colin. He phoned me first thing this morning. He got out of bed and when he looked down at his leg, all the water on his knee was gone!"

The next moment, in came Colin.

"Mark, look at this!" He rolled up his trouser leg and there was no sign of any fluid; his knee was completely normal.

News of Colin's healing soon spread down to our head office in Belfast. It so happened that the previous month, our branch had experienced a particularly good volume of sales – so good in fact that the general manager decided to come to our branch in Campsie to thank everyone and show his appreciation by taking the whole office out for a meal. While we were eating in the restaurant, the general manager turned to me and said,

"So, Mark, I heard what happened to Colin."

"What did you hear?"

"Well, I heard that you healed him."

"No, I didn't heal him. Jesus healed him."

At this point Colin took up the story, while Liam kept enthusiastically interjecting with comments like, "It's true" and "I was there" and "I saw it happen."

The general manager said, "I've got bad knees as well, and bad hips through playing rugby, and also a bad neck through a whiplash injury I sustained in a car accident."

"Really?" I said. "Would you like me to pray for you after lunch that God would also heal you?"

"Would you?"

"Sure."

So after lunch we went into the training room at the back where I'd prayed for Colin, only this time the whole office came in to witness what God was going to do, and as the general manager sat in the chair he was instantly and completely healed of all the things that were wrong in his body. He was quite literally dumbstruck and became so emotional that, in an effort not to break down in front of everyone, he shot out of the room, jumped into his car and drove all the way back down to Belfast. Everyone was completely nonplussed because that afternoon we were scheduled to have a training session with him!

As the good news of what God had done spread, it wasn't unusual for me to come into work to find people already there, waiting for me to pray for them. Waiting for me one morning was one of the company's top fitters.

"Mark, I'm in agony. I was lifting one of these big laminated windows with another fitter. I shouldn't have attempted to do it, because it really needed five of us to lift it, but I just wanted to get it done. Anyway, my back went and now I can hardly walk, let alone lift anything. The pain is so bad that I can't work and if I can't work I'm not going to earn anything. Could you please pray for me?"

"Of course I can! Let's go into the back room."

The instant I prayed for this man, God came and healed him. He was so thrilled and amazed, he got on the phone and started telling everyone, including his team of fitters, what God had done for him and that he was coming straight back to work!

I certainly learnt some skills working for that double-glazing company and all the time God was giving me new perspectives on healing.

When Linda and I arrived in Northern Ireland we worshipped

with the church in Coleraine that had been instrumental in helping us to come over. Sadly, things didn't really work out there and after about a year we left, knowing that this wasn't the place where God wanted us to be.

Looking back now, I can see that it was a stepping stone for us. But at the time I was quite depressed. I thought I'd blown it. I'd left revival back in Westminster and was finding the transition to Northern Ireland really difficult.

I had no idea why I was there and I didn't like the house we were renting at the time. Linda, on the other hand, was at home straight away, even though I felt it was much harder for her because she'd left her parents and all her family behind in England. Knowing she and the boys were so much behind me blew me away, but paradoxically it also made me feel even worse.

One evening, when I was feeling particularly sorry for myself, I sat down on the worn and evil-smelling sofa in our rented home, when a spring came through the seat and ripped into my best trousers. From the moment of that spring going into my backside, God began dealing with some areas of my life that needed it. He didn't waste time in refining my character to prepare me for what was to come and I felt him stirring me up in places where I didn't realise I needed stirring up.

Even though that sofa had seen better days my reaction should have been one of gratitude, but instead I was moaning and complaining. God had to teach me how to learn to be content in each and every situation. He had already dealt with me about cars, because I was a little bit of a snob where they were concerned. I was given an old Vauxhall Vectra, but before I became a Christian I wouldn't have even deigned to sit in such a car, let alone drive one!

There were many rough edges of my character that needed knocking off, and that spring provoked something in me, so that God could deal with it.

As time went on, and we still hadn't found a permanent place to worship, I began to question more and more why I was in Northern Ireland at all. I hadn't really wanted to move there in the first place, God had told me to lay my public ministry down, and the only job I could find was that of a double-glazing salesman.

Either God has a sense of humour, I thought, or I've blown this big time. I'd been going to lots of different churches and things finally came to a head one Sunday morning when I found myself sitting in yet another church. I started doubting everything. I doubted ever hearing from God in the first place and I felt I'd made a huge mistake. So I prayed:

"God, if I've made a mistake, then let me find out where I've gone off track. I'm here because I want to follow you and be obedient to you, so Lord, I need your help. Please give me some indication or some sign that I'm doing the right thing."

On one of my early visits to Coleraine, I'd been presented with a beautiful leather-bound Bible which I'd never actually used. In fact it was still in the box it came in. I'd never taken it out of its box, even when it was first given to me. I'd simply thanked the church for such a lovely gift and stuck it on the bookshelf at home. But for some reason, on this particular Sunday before I went to church, I decided to take the Bible out of its box and I went to church thinking I should use this new Bible.

Sitting in church, I couldn't even listen to the message. I was crying out to God,

"Please help me. I'm here in obedience to you, but I need your help."

I opened the Bible I'd been given and there, tucked in between the leaves, was a photograph that I'd never seen before. It had been placed in there when the church presented the Bible to me. It was a photograph of Linda and myself that had been taken in May 1994 whilst on a tent mission in Coleraine.

That particular visit to Coleraine was significant to me, because as I was preaching in the tent a white dove flew in through a gap in the top and perched above me. I didn't see it, but everyone was staring, and as I turned to see what everyone was staring at, the dove flew out the same way it had come in.

We were supposed to have held that mission in the Town Hall, which had been newly rebuilt after the IRA bombing in 1992, but as it wasn't completely finished the council paid for us to have a tent in the field beside the Rose Gardens in Anderson Park instead.

I also recalled the presence of a dove on my pre-mission visit to a church in the town earlier the same year. I flew back to England on the Saturday, but in the Sunday service, when the people I'd prayed for on that pre-mission visit came to tell about their healing, a white dove flew up in the church windows behind them. Everyone could see the dove at the window behind them as they stood to testify.

I gazed at this photograph of Linda and I, taken in the field where the tent mission had been held. Timothy was a baby in a pushchair and Linda and I were arm in arm, and in the background, across the road behind us, was the shop front of the company I was working for as a double-glazing salesman. That particular branch had since closed, so when I looked at the photograph I knew God had set me up. This was his way of letting me know that everything was right on track. I really was in the right place.

"Thank you God," I whispered. That was all I needed, as I put the photo back into the pages and closed the Bible.

I was with that double-glazing company for four years, but this was part of a six-and-a-half year wilderness period in my life. I had felt God say to me,

"Mark in the past you've gone wherever you wanted to go, and I've come with you, but no more. Now I'm going to take you by the hand and I'm going to lead you and you're to come with me. You're to go through the doors I open. Do not push any doors. I'm going to do a new thing."

I didn't really know what God meant by that, but during this time I heard about Alan and Kathryn Scott planting a Vineyard church on the Causeway Coast. Coincidentally, they came over to Coleraine in the same week, month and year as Linda and I did, but I didn't know anything about them or about the Vineyard. In the past I had gone along to some John Wimber conferences, which had given me a great respect for the man, and I loved all that God was doing through him, but I knew nothing of the Vineyard movement of churches he was credited with starting.

So because I was looking for a place where people didn't really know me and I could be obedient to God without anyone pressurising me to preach or minister, I went to see Alan and Kathryn and told them what I felt God had said to me about laying down my public ministry. They encouraged me to come along and worship with them, with no expectation that I would have to do a single thing.

I felt a great sense of relief. Meeting at the Edgwater Hotel on a Sunday, overlooking the sea, and with Kathryn leading worship, it was like heaven opening up and I knew this was where God wanted me. At last I felt as though I'd found my spiritual home and those early years were a precious time of healing for me.

I experienced inner healing for some past relational hurts and brokenness and came into a new freedom and confidence to be the person God had made me to be. I knew there was a gifting and anointing on my life and being with the Scotts allowed me the freedom to simply be myself, without feeling pressurised or squeezed to fit into a mould that others had for me.

I was also in need of some physical healing. By now I'd been working for four years as a double-glazing salesman and I'd injured my back through lugging all the heavy bags around and constantly lifting them in and out of the boot of my car. The pain was so bad that it was excruciating and my doctor told me I would have to change my profession. I took his advice and since Linda had recently started a small part-time business which was doing well, I quit my job with the double-glazing company and began to help her.

I would love to say that God healed me, but my back just got better when I started going to the gym and taking physical exercise. What people often fail to realise with physical healing, is just how important maintaining your health is. I regularly go to the gym and try and watch what I eat, because I want longevity in ministry. I've met lots of people whose spirit is willing, but whose flesh is burnt out, so I'm trying to learn the secret of the balance between proper rest, exercise and diet.

8

ON THE STREETS WITH THE VINEYARD

⁕

Within a couple of years of being with the Scotts, God told me to "Get ready". Confirmation of this came in a prophetic word I received about a genesis, a time of new beginnings. These were encouraging words for me because I'd been chomping at the bit to get out and do things.

Then Alan came to me and said,

"Mark, we're going to be doing some things out on the street. You don't have to do anything, but if you feel like you want to do something, we'd love you to come along."

We took a few chairs out and started inviting people to come for healing. It wasn't the Healing on the Streets model as such; I still didn't have any real clarity about that, for me it was just about getting out there!

Alan was a little nervous about taking something he was inexperienced in out onto the streets. I had explained to him the basic format of what I used to do in the past, which was to go into town centres and make an evangelistic proclamation, whereupon people would gather, healing would occur, and people would then testify to what had happened. So I took a lead and, as I began to do that, people started to gather.

An Indian lady with arthritis came and sat in one of the chairs. She had one leg shorter than the other. I shouted out,

"If you want to see a miracle, come."

I think at this point Alan began to panic. He was still getting to know me and had just heard some stories. He was most probably thinking, "No! We don't do that. Help! I've just released some crazy guy onto the streets!"

A crowd started to gather and I prayed for this woman's leg to grow. The leg grew out and her knees were healed of arthritis. After publicly testifying to her healing, she walked away with her daughter very happy indeed. When they'd got about fifty yards down the road, Alan ran after them, thinking to himself that people from their culture will say they're healed even if they're not, just so as not to embarrass you. He just wanted to be sure.

When he caught up with them, he said,

"You can tell me if you weren't really healed. It's okay, you can tell me."

The daughter was really indignant and replied,

"Excuse me, my mother is completely healed!"

Alan was more surprised that the woman had been healed than she was, but he was thrilled nonetheless. Then others began to get healed. In particular there seemed to be a healing anointing at that time for bad backs, broken bones and arthritic conditions.

It takes strong and courageous leadership to do what Alan and Kathryn did that day. They took a big risk with me. Alan and Kathryn are amazing leaders, willing to risk it all for God and for the sake of their city. God loves and responds to this kind of brave leadership. It marks them out and the fruit of their leadership is plain for all to see. I could not be where I am now without their love, trust and investment in my life, and I am indebted to them.

Alan told his friend Jamie Watters from the Glasgow Vineyard church about some of the things that we were seeing God do and so Jamie invited me over to lead a weekend for the church and take them out to pray for healing on the streets of Glasgow.

God was already giving me insight into some things and, in embryonic form, the Healing on the Streets model was beginning to take shape in my mind. In those days I would use an amplified mic and begin sharing stories of healing I had experienced. I would then ask anyone who stopped to listen and who was sick if we could pray for them.

At Jamie's church they had seen some healings but it was sporadic, and not in the experience of the majority of their congregation. I spoke at the church on the Sunday evening and when it came to the ministry time, I asked if anyone in the congregation had one leg shorter than the other.

Unbeknown to me, there was a student geologist called Caroline in the congregation. She was on the verge of cancelling a skiing holiday because she had just come through an operation for two fused discs in her back and was in agony, barely able to bend down without considerable pain. Before the operation the church had prayed for her several times and although the Spirit would come upon her and the pain would reduce, it would always come back again a couple of days later.

Her parents booked her into a private hospital and she had an operation on her back which addressed the fused disc condition. During her stay in hospital she was diagnosed as having one leg about an inch shorter than the other. The week she was discharged the podiatrist and physiotherapist recommended an insert for her shoes. She had just been measured for these two days previously and the inserts had been ordered.

So when I made the call for anyone who had one leg shorter than the other, Caroline responded. Wanting to build faith in the congregation, I announced,

"If you've never seen a miracle before, then please come to the front and gather round Caroline and watch what God is going to do with her legs."

The poor pastor was thinking, "This had better work or I'll have a lot of clearing up to do here."

The whole congregation came forward, including the most vocal and ardent atheist on the university campus, who had only come along to ridicule the Christian students in the church who believed in a God who heals today. She came and stood within inches of Caroline and stared intently at her legs.

I sat Caroline down in a chair, measured the length of her legs by holding her heels together in my hands and then prayed a prayer of command. The shorter leg shot forward instantly until it was the same length as the other one. Caroline said she could feel it stretching and when she stood up her knees were perfectly level and all the pain from her operation had gone.

Jamie came and spoke to the now dumbstruck, so-called atheist, and asked her what she had experienced. In a state of shock, all she could say was,

"I saw and now I believe."

The Spirit of God came on her and some of the other students in the church led her to the Lord that evening and she joined the church family. The church experienced over fifty healings that weekend and Caroline's healing in particular fuelled something in the community there.

Because I knew something of John Wimber's ministry, I thought that all Vineyard churches would be experiencing signs and wonders, but Jamie assured me this was not the case. He said it would be really helpful if I could develop what I was doing into a teaching and equipping format that had both theory and practice. He saw that given a little development and theological grounding, this could become a vehicle for training and equipping people for the healing ministry.

One of the highest values in the Vineyard church movement is equipping the saints. As John Wimber would say, "Everyone gets to play" meaning that the ministry of the Holy Spirit is available to the laity and not just the pastors and leaders.

So Jamie sowed the seed in my mind about a training manual incorporating both information and demonstration. That idea really stirred me, because anything to do with equipping the Church was where I felt God was calling me to invest. I had a heart to encourage others to do what I was doing. I wanted to cause their faith to rise and take them by the hand, lead them out and show them how to do it. I knew I had an anointing for healing, but I also had a passion and anointing for encouraging others to do the same.

The thought had been germinating in my mind for a few weeks and then, over a three-day period, I suddenly had this divine download as I sat at the computer and began to type out the bare bones of Healing on the Streets. I could see it as clear as day and I began to add meat to the bones. Much of it was wisdom from all my experiences of the past in street evangelism, but with some fresh insights and from a totally different perspective.

One of the great successes of Healing on the Streets has been that it brings churches of different streams together, but that wasn't in my thinking at the time. It was only much later that God gave me the reasons why the model enabled churches from both ends of the spectrum to work together. I could see that it was like bringing the pendulum into the centre where everyone could agree to run with this model.

The Lord had told me to get ready and now I had a few dozen pages of this manual in skeletal form. Being an evangelist, I thought I ought to include something about leading people to Jesus, but I felt an emphasis of this ministry was to teach the Church how to be carriers of God's presence and how to release God's Kingdom with authority onto the streets. So I left that out, thinking that every church should be teaching their people how to lead people to Jesus anyway.

After my visit to the Glasgow Vineyard, the church started going out on the streets and news spread about the healings they were seeing. As a consequence, in 2005 Jamie was invited to teach a healing workshop at the Vineyard National Leaders' Conference in Bournemouth. As my visit to their church had been catalytic for them, Jamie invited me to join him to teach at the conference and lead some teams onto the streets.

I felt God had already said to me that he was going to open a door, so I gladly accepted his invitation. The evening before the final day of the conference, I was in my hotel room and in the middle of the night I woke up to the most incredible encounter with God I've ever had. The room was filled with an incredible sense of God's presence and I was overwhelmed with an experience of his fatherly "abba" love for me. I was his child, he was my dad and I felt safe and secure and totally accepted.

I don't know how long that lasted, but it felt like half an hour before I fell asleep then woke a second time to an awareness of the awesome presence of God filling the room. So intense was his closeness that I was afraid to open my eyes in case I saw him. I experienced a God of such immense power and authority and holiness and purity, but also the King of kings and Lord of lords. I was so in awe of God that his presence made me quake.

Then I fell asleep again and the Lord woke me up a third time. This time he showed me the enemy's plan for my life which really shook me. Once more I fell asleep and then a fourth time God woke me and he showed me his plan for my life, which again really shook me!

That profound encounter with Jesus radically shaped my understanding of what this was becoming. I realised the significance of what it was I was carrying and what I was supposed to be doing with my life, and it positioned me to be ready for whatever it was that was coming.

When the final day of the conference came we went out onto the streets of Bournemouth and we had this little banner which simply read "Healing" and a few chairs spaced out in a row. A gang of youths began to heckle and shout, so we sent some people over to quieten them down while we prayed for people who got healed and we led people to Jesus. It was an amazing time. Many people with backaches walked away pain-free and a lady with a skin condition and a rash all over her body was totally and instantly healed.

Many of the Vineyard churches started to become more outward-focused as a result of that conference and invitations now began to come from other church leaders asking me to come and teach their people how to minister healing on the streets.

After the conference Alan Scott came to me and said,

"Mark, up until now we've been mostly ministering to Christians who've come to us with unresolved hurts and pain, but God has said to us that, 'if we will go after the lost, he will look after the church'. So that's what we're going to do."

The church leaders felt that God was inviting us into a covenant with him and we took it seriously. Alan began to skilfully steer the church step by step, showing them that as a leadership this was where we felt God was taking us. People who didn't feel comfortable with that were released to move on, but it was clear to everyone that everything we were going to do from now on was going to be designed around reaching those outside.

This was music to my ears. It made my heart sing, because everything that Alan said I had been crying out for. Suddenly, I realised I'd found a place where the whole heart of the church was for outside its walls and I felt as though I was in heaven.

So now I was really ready to do something. I went to see Alan about launching Healing on the Streets in Coleraine, wondering how far I'd be able to go.

"How about once every two weeks," I tentatively suggested.

Initially Alan didn't respond, so I ventured, "Maybe once a month?"

He looked at me intently and said, "How about once a week?"

I'd felt that had been too much to ask, but this was exactly what I wanted to do.

"That'd be just great!"

"Okay. As God's given you the picture for how this should look, then let me know what you need. Whatever it is you want, we'll provide it."

So the church invested in some basic equipment: six sturdy

wooden chairs, a tall banner and a portable PA system. Then one Saturday morning during Easter 2005, we launched Healing on the Streets in Coleraine to connect with our community and reach out to men and women of all ages and backgrounds, to really make a difference in their lives.

9

BOWING THE KNEE
TO JESUS

Before the launch of the first Healing on the Streets, we invited anyone from the church who was interested to sign up for two Sunday evenings of basic training. Many of those who came along had never seen healing before and one couple, Philip and Maxine McCluskey, only came to the training because they were acting as a taxi service for their daughter who had signed up. They decided to stay, feeling that they might learn some skills which would be useful to them in the running of their small group.

I decided to teach the assembled group how words of knowledge work, because I wanted to show that all the gifts of the Spirit can flow through the healing ministry, not just healing. I asked the Lord to show me a few things about people there and I felt that there were two women who'd had phobias of the dark since childhood. I invited them to come to the front if they wanted God to set them free.

Maxine and another woman stood up and came to the front

where I led them in a prayer. Both of them fell to the floor under the power of God and were deeply impacted. Coming from a traditional church background, Philip was surprised to see God move in a way that he'd never experienced before, and he was even more surprised when his wife was healed. When I announced that the following Saturday morning we were going onto the streets of Coleraine, Philip and Maxine were shocked. They knew the training was called Healing on the Streets, but they never thought it meant that we were literally going to go out to do it on the streets!

Nevertheless, they came out as part of the team on that very first morning, and although they were quite fearful, they were amazed that people came and sat on the chairs in the middle of Coleraine and asked for prayer. Philip had never had any previous experience of praying for people to be healed and he felt a mixture of fear and excitement, but found he really enjoyed it.

After that first week, Philip was hooked. He discovered that whenever he went out on the streets God would do something new. More and more people kept coming and more and more got healed. Philip's confidence grew to the point where he knew that if he would turn up, then so would God. As he experienced God working through him, and as he saw people healed of various sicknesses, his excitement grew, so that he was unable to stop doing it, and now he and Maxine lead the Coleraine Healing on the Streets team.

In fact, many of the team had never seen the sick healed or been used by God in this way before.

As they went out, they were astonished to see that God could use them. They've consistently seen the sick healed, lives transformed, people led to faith in Jesus Christ, and the power of God at work in broken and hurting lives.

Some of the team is now comprised of people who we met on the streets, who didn't know Jesus, but needed healing. They responded and came to the chairs for prayer, they were healed and then started going to church. Along the way they accepted Christ, began to attend a small group and when the next Healing on the Streets training sessions were running, they went to them and are now on the streets with us, also ministering to the sick and leading others to Jesus.

On the day we launched Healing on the Streets the team stood in a circle to pray. The early morning shoppers looked at us quizzically as they passed by. We had spaced the chairs, hoisted the healing banner into place, music was playing gently in the background, and everything was ready. We needed God's presence and I will never forget how one of the team prayed that day:

"Lord, may the people of Coleraine, and those visiting our town, bow their knee to you."

Immediately I felt my heart being challenged by the Holy Spirit: "But what about you Mark, are you willing to bow the knee?" This was an invitation not just to bow the knee to him, but to join with Jesus the servant King. Together we knelt down on the paving in Coleraine's Diamond Square outside the Town Hall.

What happened next was amazing.

We know that God is at work out on the streets, but he's been waiting for a long time for his people to join him in what he's doing. God's presence was already on the streets that day, but as we knelt on the ground it felt like a huge wave of his tangible presence was released into the Square, filling the whole area.

You could feel the rush of God's Spirit and hear the town hush to the arrival of God's kingdom.

Many teams who were interested in the HOTS model had travelled over to Coleraine and asked if they could join us at the start for prayer and then observe the ministry. But many didn't realise that we knelt on the pavement to pray. As we stood in a circle I welcomed our guests, introduced them to our team and then said, "Okay, let's pray!" As we dropped to our knees I observed amongst some of our visiting friends what I call the "Yo-yo" effect. It's interesting the battle that goes on inside some of us, even with the simple act of publicly kneeling before God. But time and again, when people visit us and kneel in public they experience a breaking, like the tearing of the curtain that releases the presence of God from within. For some this experience is overwhelming and they don't want to leave the ground! It's like Peter, James and John wanting to set up camp on the Mount of Transfiguration.

Wherever we have launched HOTS the experience for many going out onto the streets for the first time has been the same. We always start by kneeling together in a group in front of the chairs and banner, and lean into God. We pray quietly and corporately, asking for the increase of God's presence in the area. We ask for God's kingdom to come in power.

In the act of kneeling, not only are we expressing our submission to Jesus, our Lord, but we are expressing our humility and dependence on him for everything that happens. We either remain on our knees until his presence comes or we go home, because there's no point in doing anything if his presence isn't present. Nothing happens without his presence! The good news is that we don't have to wait long. As soon as our knees touch the ground God's presence pours out. When his presence comes there's also a sense of urgency, almost as if God is saying, "Okay, you can get up now. I've been waiting here a lot longer than you have. Let's get going!"

We must have looked a rather strange little bunch of people, all bowing down. Many times passers-by were heard to say,

"What are they doing?"

And I once heard the reply, "I think one of them has lost their contact lens!"

It took a while to take off, but every week people came to the chairs and people were healed. So much so, that by the fourth week we ended up on the front page of the local newspaper, The Chronicle, with a photograph of me holding a walking stick, under the headline, "Miracles on our Streets".

The walking stick had been given to me as a "souvenir" by a 78-year old ex-marine called Daniel who'd come to the chairs for prayer. Daniel had a number of things wrong with him, but the thing that hurt him the most was that he was no longer able to march because of the pain in his leg and hip.

As he sat in the chair and we began to pray, the Spirit of God rested on him and tears filled his eyes as he could feel God touching his leg and his hip. When he got up off the chair he was in a state of wonder and amazement at the dawning realisation that God had healed him. He got up and tried out his brand new leg. All the pain had gone and for half an hour he stood telling everyone within earshot that God had healed him and he would no longer be needing a stick to walk with.

In those early days of Healing on the Streets in Coleraine there was a man called John who would turn up every Saturday we were there. He would just watch us and hang around, but always refused our invitation to receive any prayer.

John was well known in the local motorbiking community and over the course of a year we got to know him really well. It was obvious he just loved being there and I believe he was being ministered to by God's presence in that place.

John had a liking for good quality coffee, so when we started making tea and coffee for the team around noon, we made sure we had good coffee to give him. We discovered that he also liked chocolate-chip cookies from Marks and Spencer's. Since my personal favourite was their pistachio cookies, buying chocolate-chip cookies for John gave me the excuse I needed to treat myself each week to the pistachio ones!

In those early days, before I began travelling so much, I was always with the team outside the Town Hall in Coleraine. My job was to get everything we needed packed up in the car ready to go out. On wet days, of which there were many in Northern Ireland, in addition to the chairs, banner and PA, that meant umbrellas, paper kitchen towels and a plastic bin liner to cover the PA to keep it from getting wet. I usually pulled one bag off a reel I kept at home.

On this particular Saturday though, for some reason, I'd pulled off three bags from the reel. Being in a hurry, I covered the PA with one and just stuffed the other two into my jacket pocket.

Outside the Town Hall, I watched the team on my left, who were all kneeling down and praying for a paranoid schizophrenic who was hooked on marijuana, while the team to my right were kneeling and praying for a young man with Tourette's. The teams were gently and compassionately ministering to these two men with great tenderness. Despite the steady rain that was falling, I stood there, thinking to myself that things couldn't get much better than this, when a man in his late forties started to come towards me. He was in a terrible state, covered from head to foot in dried vomit, and he came and sat down in the chair beside me and said,

"I have no one to speak to, but I know I can speak to you."

As I knelt down by his side he began to share how he had lost everything – his wife, his children, his business and his home – and now by implication only his life was left. From the inside of his jacket he pulled out a bottle of poitín (pronounced pochine), which is the illegal Irish alcohol made from fermented potato peelings. It will literally turn you blind. Whatever was in the bottle looked disgusting and my heart went out to him, most probably because my father was an alcoholic.

As I was kneeling in front of him, sharing God's love with him, he suddenly began to retch and his vomit went all over me. The stench was appalling and my stomach began to heave. The man apologised profusely. He was so embarrassed because he did try to warn me, but his warning came too late.

"Don't worry," I said. "Nothing's changed. God loves you with all of his heart. You just stay there. You'll be okay. We have kitchen roll to clear this up."

And then I realised why I had those two extra bags in my pocket and as he still hadn't finished vomiting, I gave them to him and he began to fill them up. It really was disgusting! I looked over my shoulder for some support from the rest of the team, only to find they'd all scattered to the four winds. But standing there, two feet away, listening to every word I was saying to this man was John, and he was watching me closely to see what I was doing.

I managed to wipe the sick off me and off the pavement and off this man, and dispose of the bags and then I went back and knelt down beside him and again began to reaffirm God's love towards him. I had unfortunately missed some sick that had gone down his sleeve and as he put his arm round my neck to hug me, I could feel the cold sick sticking to the back of my neck. As he embraced me, I began to pray my best prayer, and when I had finished, the rain came and washed away all traces of the vomit.

I didn't realise that I still smelt quite bad, but when I got home Linda said,

"What on earth is that smell?"

God spoke to me then and gave me yet another revelation of his unfathomable love for me and for people. I knew God hated sin, but I never really knew how sin actually affected him, and he was trying to explain to me on a human level that it's like the worst smell you've ever smelt. It's a stench to his nostrils. The sort of smell that makes you gag. A smell so disgusting you wouldn't want to take another breath. Yet when I was steeped in the stench of that, Jesus willingly stepped into it to rescue me, and then God spoke to me and said,

"Mark, this is what it's going to take if you're going to reach those on the outside. You will need to be able to love the unlovable – the people who you'd rather cross to the other side of the road to avoid; to love them unconditionally. You will need to embrace those whose shame is very visible and to hide and cover their shame with the Father's love, and go hands and knees into someone else's mess to help them clear it up. That's what it's going to take. Are you willing?"

"Yes, Lord," I whispered, "I'm willing."

Then the next day, John, for the first time, came into church and the following Saturday when we knelt on the ground to pray, I felt someone quietly kneel down next to me and when I opened my eyes it was John. He was making a statement and it was so powerful. It was such a beautiful thing. John's now gone to be with the Lord, but it was so worthwhile to kneel down in the cold and the rain, week in, week out, for a whole year, just for him.

It's an awesome experience and privilege to kneel on the streets with Jesus, and even more so when there are miraculous signs and supernatural interventions. On one occasion on a chilly Saturday morning as we knelt to pray, we hadn't been praying for long when the quietness was broken by a boisterous noise. As I looked up I saw a group of teenagers dressed in football gear. These boys formed a local football team who met each Saturday to play football, but disappointingly as they met together that morning they realised that so many of them were carrying injuries they couldn't play.

One of the boys said to the rest of the team, "Get into your football gear and come with me, we're playing football!" This boy had previously seen two of his friends healed in front of his eyes during HOTS. One of his friends had an abnormal bone growth below the knee so that it resembled a camel's hump. He stood in shock as he watched the "hump" disappear from his friend's leg. Eventually he also came for prayer and experienced healing, so he knew exactly where to bring his injured pals. As we stood to our feet the seats quickly filled with these injured footballers. Soon we were praying and every single one of those boys was healed on the spot. I just love the way God healed these kids so that they could go and enjoy their game of football.

The writer to the Hebrews says: "Let us fix our eyes on Jesus, the author and perfecter of our faith, who for the joy set before him endured the cross." (Hebrews 12:2)

As we kneel we are coming again to the foot of the cross and fixing our eyes upon Jesus. Everything looks different from the perspective of the cross. It causes us to look outwards. It shows us a dying, hurting world in need of a Saviour and reminds us why Jesus came.

Jesus' mission on earth was "to seek and to save what was lost" (Luke 19:10), and his Great Commission for the church is to continue this. Jesus' gaze is always outwards and when we follow him, he leads us out, just as he said to his first disciples in Matthew 4:19: "Come follow me, and I will make you fishers of people."

When we kneel again at the foot of the cross out on the streets, we gain the right perspective and we rise empowered.

10

THE HEALING ON
THE STREETS MODEL

As I write, there's a stirring in the Church to return to its original design and purpose in the world. God's plan and strategy is to bring his Church back in line with its original calling of fulfilling the great commission, but with an understanding of our royal priesthood. We are God's children, citizens of the kingdom, with delegated authority that comes from being ambassadors of the King. We are trusted rulers.

God wants us out of our buildings and back on the streets. He is moving us from fear to faith. He wants us to have an unshakeable faith that's rooted in truth, demonstrated through prayer and action, that rocks the face of the impossible.

To get us to this place, God is releasing creative models to help us break out and break free, until the Church finds her "feet" and we begin to do what should come naturally to every believer. The Church is looking for guidance; a simple model for everyone that's workable, sustainable and relevant. HOTS is a model that is helping the Church step out to those who would never step in; to reach out to those who would never reach in. It's a specific model to connect the local church to its community on the streets. It enables churches in an area to come together and work together, using a method of prayer and an approach that everyone can agree on.

We use a banner, chairs, music and leaflets. These are just the "props" which help us to facilitate and establish a regular healing ministry on the streets, and releases the church to engage with its community, building relationships over the long term. We know God can do this without any "props," but churches are in need of simple steps to help them on their outward journey.

The HOTS model is simple yet profound, gentle yet powerful, full of God's presence and brimming over with love. It's accessible and safe for every believer to learn to engage with their community. It brings the atmosphere of Heaven into a location and creates a place of healing there, allowing ordinary people the opportunity of experiencing the kingdom and encountering the King.

HOTS has a look and feel which distinguishes it from other models people may have experienced in the past. We create an environment on the streets that spreads the fragrance of Jesus and brings the hush and awe of Heaven to anyone walking through the area, whether they sit on our chairs or not! It's unpressurised and peaceful. It's an oasis of healing where people are offered the opportunity to drink from the fountain of life.

We build relationships over time, creating stepping stones that allow people who are far away from God to come to Jesus and be healed along the way. This gentle, non-confrontational ministry works within a loving and compassionate environment, full of the presence and power of the Holy Spirit. It is marked by a true sense of peace. Amongst the hustle and bustle of busy shoppers walks the Prince of Peace. The kingdom comes; stillness falls; passers-by begin to slow and stop as the deepening presence of God draws their hearts. As people are drawn to the chairs and take a seat, we gather around each one in groups of two to four to kneel and pray our best prayer. God has given us something that's fresh, simple and within the reach of every believer. No one ever prays alone, but always together in a group.

HOTS is not an extension or an add-on or just another church programme. It is a beautifully simple way to regularly reach out to the lost and hurting on the streets of our community.

I saw that the model would work best in locations where the greatest number of people pass by during the busiest times of the day. In Coleraine, the ideal spot is outside the Town Hall where there is a pedestrianised square with shops on either side. Many people are coming and going. It's a highly visible location and there's a lot of space.

Any shopper can see our large banner from a long way off because it measures 5.3 metres tall by one metre wide! You can hardly miss it. Printed on the banner from top to bottom and behind a modern blue graphic background is the word HEALING in large white lettering. We have a small church logo printed at the bottom. Gone are the days when I write "Healing and Miracles" in my poor handwriting on a sketch board!

The giant pole banner takes us about ten minutes to assemble on site. It has a 70 litre base that we've filled with heavy gravel. In Coleraine the wind whips around the town and it can knock any sign over, so it needs to be pretty sturdy.

We space six wooden chairs out in a line, three on either side of the banner with 5-6ft of space between each chair to allow a team of two to four people to pray around each chair without interfering with the team praying for the person in the adjacent chair. Even when we have only a small team, I still put out all six chairs as a statement of faith. The chairs are sturdy enough to hold the weight of the largest person comfortably, with no armrests to get in the way and a tall back for comfort.

In the first six months of doing HOTS in Coleraine our team gave out 50,000 professionally printed fliers to everyone passing by. On one side of the A6 flier is printed the word "Healing" in modern graphics to match the banner, and on the other side is the following statement:

"We believe God loves you and can heal you from back or neck pain, arthritis, depression, chronic pain, sleeping problems, smoking, allergies, headaches, walking difficulty, lung problems, anxiety, digestive problems, chest pain or any other physical or emotional condition.

Take a seat and we'll pray for you, it's completely free! We offer prayer between 10.30am and 1.00pm each Saturday outside Coleraine Town Hall, whatever the weather. We're followers of Jesus from Causeway Coast Vineyard church."

In Northern Ireland we have to prepare for all kinds of weather because we're on the streets every Saturday, come rain or shine, and more often than not it's the rain that comes! Waterproof containers keep our fliers and literature dry and we take large umbrellas to cover the people being prayed for. Kitchen roll ensures that wet chairs are nicely dry before people sit down and flasks of hot water allow us to make tea and coffee on site for the team in cold weather and for anyone coming for prayer.

In Coleraine we have to be prepared for the freezing cold as well as the wet, which means that the team has to be well equipped with thermals as well as waterproof clothing. In the winter I have sometimes needed to wear three layers of thermals! The weather is not a hindrance to God, however, and is never an excuse for us not to go out. People come for prayer no matter the weather and we would be letting them down if we weren't there.

The model works best when we turn up every week at the same place at the same time. It creates momentum and people always know you'll be there regardless of the weather. We never leave before the time printed on our fliers, because we've seen that time and time again people come for prayer at the last minute and are so relieved to find us still there, even if we are packing things away!

We meet half an hour before we start to set up and spend some time praying. Then we hand out our healing fliers to anyone passing by. This is a personal invitation for them to come and take a seat if they are sick, and if people stop and show interest we engage them in conversation and invite them to accompany us to one of the chairs where we can pray for them.

We also have a small modern outdoor PA system that we use to play some gentle contemporary instrumental Christian music. The music helps people to relax and engage with God's presence on the streets.

The team who've been through the training course then minister to anyone who takes a seat, whilst others continue to hand out fliers to passers-by and engage people in conversation as the opportunity arises.

Two to four of our team will go over to those taking a seat, the men to pray with men and the women to pray with women. We introduce ourselves in a friendly way and ask the person for their name, which we use throughout the time of prayer. As we ask what they want prayer for, we are listening to them with one ear but also listening to God with the other, to see what he might be saying about the person. We're not looking for a long medical history, because we're not doctors, we just want to know what it is they want Jesus to do for them.

We then ask permission to lay our hands on them. We gently lay our hands as close as possible to the affected area, being careful only to do so if it's appropriate and they feel comfortable.

Before we begin to pray, we look the person in the eyes and begin to tell them that God loves them with all of his heart. Often the gifts of the Holy Spirit flow naturally from our hearts as we begin to express the truth of God's love towards that person and we speak out what God truly thinks of them. Many times we have seen people healed as they received the truth of God's love for them, before we have even prayed.

Our motivation for going out onto the streets is the compelling love of Christ. Whether people are healed or not, we want those who come to the chairs for prayer to be left in no doubt at all that God loves them and that here are a group of Christ-passionate people who truly care.

We begin to pray by inviting the Holy Spirit to come and reveal his presence to the person and for God to touch them with his peace and love. When we sense that the person is connecting with God, we use authoritative prayer and words of command to release healing. For example, if a person has cancer, we speak to the cancer and command it to dissolve, to disappear and go. Whatever condition a person may have we take authority over it and command the sickness, pain, disease or infirmity to go from their body.

As we pray we're also asking the Holy Spirit to give us words of encouragement and comfort to share with that person. We always pray with our eyes open and when one of the team have come to the end of whatever it is they are praying, they look to the rest of the team to see if anyone else has something to share. The team are looking to each other as well as looking to God, and often, like a tag team, the Holy Spirit will bounce things from one team member to another.

Once a man came who had growths on his bladder and shared with the team how he was mourning the death of his father. One of the team felt God wanted to speak to him from Psalm 91:4: "He will cover you with his feathers, and under his wings you will find refuge."

As he began to share this verse of Scripture, a white feather flew out of the sky and landed on the man's knee. He picked the feather up and placed it in his wallet, saying, "That's from God."

Some time later he came back to report that he'd been to see his doctor who could find no traces of the growths on his bladder. Not only had God completely healed this precious man, but he had also given him great comfort at a time of deep loss.

The Holy Spirit is our partner on the streets and we have learnt to depend on him. He longs to reach out and touch every person who goes by. He is so passionate about people! God wants to pour out his love and compassion on the streets so that people will know that there is a God who loves and cares for them.

The Bible says that it is "through us" that God "spreads everywhere the fragrance of the knowledge of him" (2 Corinthians 2:14). We are temples of the Holy Spirit. He lives in us and it's through us that the Holy Spirit flows out to touch people.

We are like the alabaster jar of perfume that the Gospels tell us was broken and poured out for Jesus. The fragrance of the perfume filled the entire house. The fragrance of the Holy Spirit has to fill our streets and it's through us that it will happen, as we allow ourselves to be broken and poured out, like that alabaster jar, for the sake of the lost – recognising that Jesus has given us his authority and he's empowered us with his Holy Spirit.

We have also learnt to pray from a place of rest. Ephesians 2:6 says that, "God raised us up with Christ and seated us with him in the heavenly realms in Christ Jesus."

Jesus has been raised to the right hand of the Father where he is seated on a throne of power and authority, and as we have also been raised with Christ we are seated with him on that throne. His throne is a place of rest and from that place Jesus exercises his authority and delegates it to us.

Ministering on the streets demands so much that we will very soon burn out if we give out of our own strength. We need to learn to draw water from the deep well of the Holy Spirit, and when we do, instead of being burnt out we are revived. The more we draw, the more we can give out. And out of the vast resources of God, instead of panic comes peace; instead of fear there is faith; instead of being stressed we are stretched, and as we are stretched we can grow.

Ministering healing is a wonderful opportunity to share God's love and compassion. In a world so full of hurting and broken people, we have to minister with the gentleness of Jesus. The way in which we minister is so vitally important. One lady who was prayed for remarked that what impacted her the most was that she experienced a "gentleness that was beyond gentle."

We should be showering people with love and compassion by the bucket load, and although we believe God can heal every sickness, disease and deformity, we'll never make a judgment on what we think God is or isn't doing in someone's life when we pray, because we aren't always able to see the healing process at work in a person's life. We can pray with confidence, knowing that Jesus heals through us, but we have to trust him and rest in him, knowing that the results of our prayers are up to him.

When we've finished praying we always ask people to test their healing out by doing something they couldn't do before. For those in pain or with some form of disability then it's easy to test out whether they have been healed, and we always encourage them to do that. But for others that might mean a visit to the doctor, and if they are taking medication we advise them not to discontinue that until they have first spoken with their doctor.

Everyone we pray for is given an A5 envelope containing a letter explaining who we are, why we've done what we've done, and some guidance on how they can pursue God further. We also include a "Why Jesus?" booklet and an invitation to our church. We are careful to ensure that all our literature is well presented and of a high quality.

For us at the very beginning, it took a while for people to come to the chairs. We had to have confidence in God that he was at work unseen, drawing people to himself. Like the farmer who has sown his seed, we had to wait patiently, knowing that the seed is germinating and will in time produce a harvest. We were in it for the long haul, so there wasn't any point in panicking.

When I'm training teams in other towns and cities, I always

encourage them to persist with the model we've developed, even though it may be slow or difficult to get things off the ground. Because of the simplicity of the model, there can be the temptation to change or complicate it. I've seen this happen for a number of reasons – discouragement, distractions, wanting to fall back on past models of evangelism, not seeing immediate results or appreciating the bigger picture.

Yet if we plough the ground and sow the seed, a harvest is sure to come. People will come to the chairs, they will respond to the leaflets; people will be returning for more prayer, and people will come because they have heard through word of mouth what God has been doing for their friends or family.

In the early days before I had an administrator, I was finding it hard to organise all the invitations that were coming in, so I prepared some guidelines for the HOTS model I was going to teach, which I'd send on ahead of my visit. These guidelines detailed all the props needed and where to get them from – the wooden chairs, the banner, the portable PA music system, the leaflets to give out and so on.

On one memorable HOTS launch in a town, not everything went to plan. I thought everything was in place and ready when I arrived, but my heart dropped when I saw that nearly every piece of equipment and material used for the ministry was not what we had recommended, and really wasn't suitable for the streets. I thought I had made it clear, but I hadn't checked. I've said this many times: I know God can do this without the props, but there's a very good reason for using high quality materials and having a high standard of presentation. This particular banner had no pole and it was over 5 metres high. It was huge!

"How are you going to display it," I asked?

"Oh, there's a high post we can tie it to."

I made a conscious decision not to allow myself to become discouraged. I would give of my best, and that evening after I had finished teaching the model I was satisfied that I had not withheld anything. As I stepped out of the building I glanced up to see someone half hanging out of the front passenger window of a car as it sped by. I saw a blur as I was hit in the throat with a raw egg. I was initially shocked at the force with which it hit me and the experience of its slimy contents running down the inside of my shirt. Someone was laughing at my expense, but I stood and praised God on the pavement. What a start!

The next day was wet, grey and looked miserable. As we went to set up on the street I could see how the day might go. Their chairs had foam seating which was soaking up the rain like a sponge. The photocopied fliers were falling apart in the wet. The huge PA wasn't working and with nothing to cover it with I thought it would probably blow up anyway. The ladder wasn't tall enough for someone to reach the top of the fixed post to tie the ridiculously long banner onto, and I could see the potential for someone to have a very nasty accident.

Eventually the banner was crudely tied by a tall man teetering on tiptoes, but the bottom of the banner lay in a roll! It was like a scene out of Fawlty Towers and any member of the public watching would have been in stitches of laughter! Without notice someone went and bought a weather-proof canopy and emptied the contents of the box onto the ground! At that point the presence and peace of God began to evaporate from me as I felt panic rise up inside. I desperately needed to pray and hide myself in God, so I held up my hands and said,

"Everybody stop. I have to pray."

The area we were in was frequented by pigeons and with all the rain that had fallen, the ground was speckled white and slimy from pigeon droppings. I looked at everyone's nice clothing and thought I couldn't possibly ask them to kneel with me, so I said,

"Look, please, I have to pray. You don't have to kneel, you can stand, but I must pray."

I was wearing light-coloured khaki trousers and I closed my eyes and knelt down in the slime. The moment my knees touched the ground, the presence of God came so thick and his peace returned. I began to rest in God again, thanking him for his presence. That was all I needed to know. I wasn't even conscious of anyone else there, because all that mattered to me was that I connected with God again. But when I opened my eyes, everyone else was kneeling down with me and all I could think was,

"Oh Lord, bless them. Their clothes will be ruined."

I thought then of my own clothes and what a mess they'd be in, but as I got up, I looked down at my trousers and they were spotless. They weren't soiled or wet. In fact, it was as if they had just been dry cleaned. As I was wondering about this, the pastor came to me and said in astonishment,

"Look at everyone's clothes, there are no marks on them at all, they're completely dry!"

Then people started coming to the chairs and sitting on the sopping sponge seats. One by one they got healed as God touched them. We had to leave for a debrief at the church while people were still receiving prayer, yet even during the debrief, people were ringing the doorbell saying,

"We've been looking for you. Are we too late for prayer?"

God spoke to me then and although I knew it in my head, he

underlined it for me yet again: props are just props. The props I've developed for the model come out of a desire for people to have the best and I want people to follow the guidelines because I believe they best facilitate this ministry. But at the end of the day Healing on the Streets isn't dependent on the props, it's dependent on God's presence. His presence is what brings his power and it's marked by a true sense of peace. It's in this environment that we pray for the sick and God in his love and mercy comes and graciously ministers his healing presence.

11

HOW HEALING COMES

Healing can come to people in a number of ways. When we pray for people on the streets we never make a promise or a guarantee that they'll be healed, but we do promise to pray our best prayer for them, and we leave the results up to God. Our best prayer, if you've been wondering what that is, is the prayer that comes from the bottom of our heart, connected to the heart of the one who is being lifted up to God. God is more concerned about the compassion in our hearts towards the person we're praying for, than the content of our prayers, even when we get it wrong!

As a young and inexperienced Christian eager to learn how to pray I remember praying for one man who came forward for healing at a meeting. The band was playing loud music, so I strained to hear what was wrong with this man. I got onto my knees, taking hold of both of his ankles and began to pray my best prayer, believing with all my heart that God would heal his ankles completely. My prayer was intentional, faith-filled and earnest. It came from my heart. I was so eager to see this man healed that I couldn't wait to see the results of my prayer. As the music subsided I jumped to my feet and asked him,

"How are your ankles? Try them out."

The man looked slightly bemused then replied, "There was nothing wrong with my ankles, it was my neck!"

"Oh!" I replied, "I'm sorry!"

"That's okay," he laughed as he turned his head from side to side, "I'm healed!"

Whenever we pray, we always ask people to test out their healing afterwards and to try and do something they couldn't do before. We teach simply that healing can come in three ways: either instantly, gradually, or, when there's no immediate sign of healing, that healing can come as they go.

Sometimes people are healed instantly and they can verify that immediately. We won't tell anyone that God has healed a person unless they themselves confirm it to be the case or their doctor confirms it later on.

Lindsay was a young woman who came for prayer with her friend, who had previously been healed through receiving a word of knowledge about a bad kidney. Five years before, Lindsay had fallen from the back of a fire engine. She had hit her head on the ground and blood began to pour out of the corner of her left eye near the tear duct, blinding her in that eye. When the doctors examined her they told her she would never see out of her left eye again.

Furthermore, a recent eye examination had shown that she had degenerative nerve damage in her right eye, which was possibly genetic. The team laid their hands over her eyes and prayed authoritatively, and the instant they took their hands away, Lindsay said she could see perfectly through her blind eye! She was totally amazed and speechless at what God had done for her.

When people have been healed instantly, they obviously let us know, but by far the commonest way healing comes is gradually. After prayer many people experience various degrees of healing, ranging from a slight to a significant improvement in their condition. They might tell us that they feel better or they have more movement, in which case we are able to tell them that God is in the process of healing them.

Mark 16:17-18 says: "And these signs will accompany those who believe: In my name ... they will place their hands on sick people, and they will get well."

Jesus said that getting well is a process, so when I pray I have the faith to believe that in some way healing is going to happen, whether it appears quickly or slowly. Some Christians are so blinkered when it comes to healing, thinking it can only happen in one way. Some have the wrong expectation that if God's going to heal at all, he'll do it instantly, but healing doesn't always come immediately. A misunderstanding of how healing comes can actually neutralise the very prayer we pray, even when we think we've prayed with faith. The moment a Christian prays, but believes nothing's happened because there's no perceptible change, they've negated the prayer of faith. They've let their prayer loose to God, they've given it wings, and now they've grabbed it by the feet and pulled it back and it's not going anywhere.

Jesus said: "I tell you the truth, if you have faith as small as a mustard seed, you can say to this mountain, 'Move from here to there' and it will move. Nothing will be impossible for you." (Matthew 17:20)

When there's no instant perceptible change this doesn't mean nothing is happening! Jesus doesn't say how long the mountain's going to take to move. It would be great if it could happen instantly and fly through the air so that everyone could see it, but Jesus said that it will truly happen if you put the faith that you have, all of it, no matter how small, into action.

The mountain could be anything. It could be a situation, a physical condition, or literally a mountain. Let's say you spoke to Mount Everest and commanded that incredibly big mountain to move and you believe with all your heart that it's going to move and Everest moves 1mm! The fact is, the mountain has moved, even though you can't perceive it with any of your five senses and there is no instrument that can measure such fine movement.

Have you ever thought about what happens to a person's body at microscopic levels when God begins to heal them? If we could see at such microscopic levels we'd see that there's nothing holding us together except invisible space. All the matter in the universe, including our bodies, is held together by God's spoken word. I believe the moment you open your mouth to exercise Christ's authority and command the body to be healed, or whatever it is that needs to be done, then those microscopic particles, atoms and molecules, accelerated by faith, excitedly begin to move in obedience to the word that's spoken until health is formed.

So when I speak to the mountain and command it to move, I believe that the mountain has moved even though it's not perceptible to the naked eye. Now if that mountain only moves 1mm a day, then the mountain is in motion; it is moving from imperception to perception.

How long it takes before the movement of the mountain becomes perceptible will vary, but a time will come when it will be possible to look at the mountain and know that it has moved. The space between imperception and perception is called faith.

We give our prayer wings and allow it to soar to God. In Psalm 5:3 King David said,

"In the morning, O Lord, you hear my voice; in the morning I lay my requests before you and wait in expectation."

To wait in faith means to wait patiently and with a sense of expectancy. It means you're intentional about seeing a change and the moment something becomes visible or there is a real sense of movement that you can see or feel – when your natural senses become aware of it – then that's like a tipping point. It may not be there completely, but you now know it's on its way.

I see this in 1 Kings 18 in the story of Elijah, who goes to the top of Mount Carmel to pray for rain. I believe the moment he opens his mouth to pray, he's intentional and expectant for rain to come, and God responds.

The sun is beating down, the air is bone dry, and suddenly it starts to evaporate the seawater and this dry air starts to fill with water vapour. So Elijah asks his servant, "What do you see?" He's expecting something to happen. He's not praying the same thing over and over again, but it's the progression of a prayer he started, and as he continues to pray and press in, earnestly and fervently, he knows the answer's coming and he gets excited. He senses a shift in the atmosphere and he can feel and smell this dry air become moist. So he asks the servant again, "What do you see?" but he still can't see anything.

Eventually the atmosphere is so full of water vapour that it cannot contain it any more and the vapour begins to condense and a cloud starts to form. At that point the servant sees a cloud forming. It's not yet rain, but it's the tipping point. Once the tipping point is reached that increases expectation, so when the servant sees it, Elijah says, "Let's run, rain is coming."

What I encourage people to do is look for any sign that might be a tipping point. A lot of Christians in particular, tend to look at what God's not doing, rather than what he is doing. Their default position and the way that they view God is wrong. Faith works in both directions. It works in the right way when we believe the right things, but it will also work in reverse, when we believe the lies that the enemy has sown.

One lie the enemy has sown that is perpetuated a lot among Christians is that it is possible to lose your healing. John 8:36 says, "So if the Son sets you free, you will be free indeed." I believe the enemy wants people to think that if they get healed then it won't last. If it's a condition that comes back, then what the person actually needs is not healing but deliverance from a spirit of affliction, since a demon cannot be healed, it has to be cast out. Sometimes though, if something comes back, it may be because the person is socially abusing their body to bring back a condition that God had actually healed them from.

Getting well or recovering after healing prayer takes time. Many of the people we pray for are healed over a period of time. When we have prayed for them, if they don't experience any immediate change, we explain how healing works and that their complete healing can come as they go on their way, or in one, two, three or more days. We always ask them to come back and let us know how they are and to return for further prayer as many times as they need to, because we want to leave them in a place of faith.

Annie from Ballymoney was diagnosed with liver cancer in February 2005. The doctors gave her 18 months to live and said there was nothing they could do for her. In June of 2005 she heard about HOTS and came to us for prayer. By this time she was seriously ill and her skin was a deep orange colour. But as the team began to minister to her, they could see with their own eyes that her colour began to change. Annie felt much better that very first time she came for prayer and she returned week after week for more prayer, each time noticing further improvement.

By the time Annie went back to her doctor, her skin was a healthy pink colour.

"Annie," he said, "If I didn't know any better, I'd say you didn't have cancer."

He ran through all the tests and gave her a thorough examination. The results came back to say that all traces of cancer were gone from her body. The doctor called her a walking miracle!

Alan from Limavady was also diagnosed with cancer and came to us for prayer in 2007. He had been diagnosed with inoperable, advanced cancer of the tongue, throat and lymph glands in his neck, and was about to commence seven weeks of radiotherapy and chemotherapy. When he was prayed for he later told us that almost immediately he felt a slight easing of his tongue, but he put it down to wishful thinking on his part and didn't say anything until he got home that same evening and found that he could swallow two gulps of Guinness at a time instead of the previous one!

Alan came for prayer every Saturday throughout his treatment and although he didn't experience any further dramatic effects, he was subsequently told by his consultants that the post-treatment results were "incredible" and "amazing" and that he was cancer-free, although he would need further monitoring. He told us that he had no doubt that the prayers had contributed greatly to his speedy recovery.

It's wonderful to work alongside the medical profession in bringing healing to people, but as we are not medically trained we counsel anyone taking medication to stay on that medication until their doctor has advised them otherwise. When people experience healing we always encourage them to go back to their doctor for confirmation. The verification of the medical profession is a great endorsement to others of what God can and will do.

Sometimes though, the medical profession can be highly sceptical. Philip and Maxine McCluskey's daughter, Nadine, was at university in England when we launched HOTS in Coleraine. For five years she had been suffering from coeliac disease, an allergy to the gluten in wheat, which is an incurable condition.

Two weeks later, when term had ended, she came home to Coleraine and came onto the streets for prayer. During prayer Nadine said she felt God had touched her and immediately said she had the urge to eat a panini, which is of course the last thing someone with her condition should do! Her mother and father, as responsible parents, were somewhat concerned that their daughter was wanting to eat something that could potentially make her very ill, but Nadine was insistent, so with fear in their hearts, but wanting to have faith, they went with her to eat a panini.

Normally within half an hour of eating any wheat product Nadine's skin would begin to react as if she was sunburnt and it would swell with lesions; she would feel sick and experience extreme fatigue. But half an hour passed, then an hour, then two hours, and there was no reaction. Nadine then felt like eating a hot cross bun. Nothing happened after eating that either, so she then just started eating sandwiches and cereals, all the things that had previously been off limits for her.

When she returned to university in England she made an appointment to see her doctor and said,

"I was prayed for on the streets of Coleraine and I've been healed, so I'd like you to run some tests."

The doctor just laughed.

"There's no cure for coeliac disease. We can control it, but we can't cure it."

Nadine was adamant about the tests, but the doctor still refused to do them, arguing that it would be a waste of money and time, so Nadine said she would pay for the tests herself, but, whatever, she wanted the results on paper. Mockingly the doctor said,

"Well, if you're cured does that mean we're going to send all the coeliac sufferers to the Causeway Coast to be prayed for?"

"That's up to you," said Nadine, "but I'd like the results please."

Very reluctantly and after much persuasion the doctor did the tests and three weeks later the test results came through negative. There was no sign of coeliac disease and Nadine remains coeliac free to this day.

Often as a person goes on their way their healing will appear, as happened in the story of the ten lepers in Luke 17:11-19. The Bible tells us that "as they went, they were cleansed."

One couple from Cavan had been on holiday in the Causeway Coast area and decided to come into Coleraine for some last minute shopping before driving home. The wife was paralysed from the waist down and in a wheelchair through having been administered an epidural during childbirth which had gone tragically wrong. There was nothing the doctors could do for her. Seeing our banner out on the streets, and feeling she had nothing to lose, she came for prayer with her husband.

After we had prayed for her she was still paralysed and there was no discernible sign of change in her condition, but as her husband drove the car home, she suddenly told him that something was happening in her legs and asked him to stop the car. As he pulled over, she jumped out of the car and started running up and down, completely healed.

The woman's testimony spread like wildfire in the community and many sick people from Cavan came for prayer as a result. We would not have known what had happened to the woman were it not for those who came from Cavan to be prayed for because of her story.

Many times though, people return to tell us that they've been healed, even though there was no sign of healing when we prayed. Afterwards, at some point, they gradually began to recover and they came back to let us know weeks or even months later.

Sometimes we need to pray for people more than once. In Mark chapter 8 we read about the story of Jesus laying his hands on the blind man at Bethsaida. After Jesus had first prayed, he asked the man whether he could see anything. When he said, "I see people; they look like trees walking around," Jesus laid his hands on him and prayed a second time, before the man's sight was completely restored.

If Jesus needed to pray more than once, there will certainly be occasions when we need to, so we always let people know that they can come back for healing prayer as many times as they like. We want to leave people in a place of faith, reassuring them that even if they're not healed it doesn't mean that God doesn't love them or that there's anything wrong with their faith. It's perfectly possible that they may experience God's healing later on.

We also have to avoid the danger of compartmentalising sickness and placing it in some grading system of difficulty. Some have developed a belief system that one kind of sickness is easier to heal than another. That's not biblical and it's not true, even though experience might indicate otherwise.

I used to believe that you had to progress in healing, starting to pray for something "easy", like a headache for instance, and moving up the scale of difficulty to something "more difficult" like a tumour on the brain. But, of course, whether it's healing a headache or a brain tumour, both are impossible without the power of God. One day God showed me my error in spectacular fashion.

Many years ago on a weekend mission trip to a church in Kings Heath, England, God taught me a lesson I will never forget. I might add this was not the HOTS model we use today, but part of my journey towards it. It was a steep learning curve in healing the sick.

This tiny church had struggled to make inroads into their community. For the past two years they had engaged in doorstep evangelism but without visible success. They were deeply discouraged and I had come alongside to help them.

Christians who allow themselves to remain under a cloud of discouragement, lose their smile.

"Mark, this is the hardest place you'll ever see. It's a tough nut to crack," they informed me, the words from their lips reinforcing the lie over their town.

"Great!" I replied, "God loves to crack tough nuts!"

Nowadays my reply is, "Uhh, yes I know."

"How do you know?" they ask.

"Well, people told me the last place I was in was the hardest place."

Silence usually follows!

I gave some simple training that was to be put into action on Saturday during the Kings Heath carnival, which was the highlight of our trip. The Kings Heath carnival is a yearly public event that takes place at the local park. The carnival travels through Kings Heath and finally ends up at the centre of the park, surrounded by many stalls displaying anything and everything from hobbies to bric-a-brac, clubs to local businesses. Hundreds of people wait in anticipation of the carnival's arrival; it's a fun family day out.

In the meantime, the public browse the stalls while they wait, or if they're brave enough they can jump onto a fairground ride called The Waltzer, which has fast spinning chariots on a rotating, undulating, platform. Our plan was to have a stall from which we could engage passers-by. When Saturday arrived we discovered to our dismay, that one small, but very important detail had been overlooked. Someone had forgotten to book the stall! By now every available stall had been taken and the organisers wouldn't allow us to set up within the stall area. Our only option was to set up outside of the stall area or go home. We were in no-man's land. The stall that was to be a helpful tool had now become a barrier, with the people we were trying to reach on the other side. I don't know if you've ever seen Christians carrying discouragement. They develop droopy mouth syndrome. I knew they felt they had blown it and they just wanted to go home.

We must have looked an isolated and lonely bunch on that day. We were about twenty yards away from the nearest stall; the public were on the other side; but how could we get them to cross over to us? Again I felt the familiar prompting of the Holy Spirit: "Heal the sick!"

We set up our portable speaker and using brightly-coloured poster paints I began to paint large words onto our sketch board: "MIRACLES AND HEALING HERE. 2.30pm. JESUS HEALS!" As I wrote, the person manning the nearest stall began to heckle us. This didn't help the way everyone was feeling. We began to play worship music and, as I looked out, I observed members of the public on the other side pretending not to be interested, but giving their watches a cursory glance. As 2.30pm approached I noticed an unusual amount of people slowing around the stalls nearest us.

I took the microphone and began to speak about God's love and power. I made the invitation for anyone who needed healing to come forward. No one moved, so I thought I'd be more specific.

Being the man of faith that I was, I announced, "If you're deaf, come!"

Again no one moved. Of course, they couldn't hear me if they're deaf, I thought to myself! Someone here has got to have something wrong with them. So I started to call out every sickness and disease I could think of, starting with what I thought would be the easiest to heal, then moving up my scale of difficulty.

"If you have a headache please come forward!"

No one moved. People were listening but not moving.

"If you suffer with pain, come!"

Still no movement, but the non-movement in them seemed to make me even bolder.

"If you have cancer come, if you're blind come, if you have an incurable disease, come, if you have a crippling disease come, Jesus can heal you!"

I reeled off every sickness and disease I knew, until I had exhausted my limited medical knowledge. I think I may have made up some non-existent conditions along the way.

Out of the corner of my eye I spotted a couple pushing a large lady in a wheelchair towards me. At that moment panic began to rise in my heart and as I turned my back towards them, I thought, "I hope they're not coming here! Maybe if I ignore them they'll just walk by."

As they got closer I began to pour out my complaint to God.

"This isn't fair God, please give me someone with a headache first, not someone in a wheelchair!"

Then suddenly they were in front of me. This couple with the large lady in the wheelchair. I wanted to disappear, but no, not even a tree to hide behind.

"We're Christians and this is our mother. She's paralysed and hasn't walked for over twelve years, but we believe God can heal her. Please pray for her."

My heart sank. In the back of my mind I was blaming God for getting me into this situation, but at least I had better pray my best prayer! The moment I laid my hand on this lady's head, I saw the people who were watching, but pretending not to watch, all lift their heads together towards me and stare. I could almost hear their inner incredulous gasps. "Huh? Does he really think this woman's going to get out of the wheelchair and walk?"

I began to pray, inviting God's presence. As the Holy Spirit rested on the lady, her body began to gently shake. The shaking increased in intensity until the whole wheelchair was shaking. It was like an old car engine starting up. Suddenly this woman shouted, "I want to walk, I want to walk!"

"Great," I replied, "get up and walk!"

Some of the team went to help lift her up by her arms, but I said, "No! Leave her alone! If God has healed her, he will give strength to her legs to get up and walk."

I had this awful picture in my mind of the team lifting her up, declaring, "You're healed, you're healed!" but with her lifeless legs dragging in the grass behind them. It was the nightmare scenario I wanted to avoid. Either God had healed this woman or he hadn't.

God's power flowed into the woman's legs. Unaided she got out of her wheelchair and walked. The people on the other side of the stalls came running and in an instant we had a crowd! "How is it possible," they asked? They watched in amazement as the lady walked up and down testing out her new legs.

A woman stepped forward out of the crowd and loudly announced, "I heard what you had to say; I've just seen that woman healed; I want to become a Christian now!"

This woman just happened to be our heckler from the nearby stall. Should you ever be publicly heckled, look at them from God's perspective. We see a heckler, but God sees an evangelist. Heckler? No, think evangelist!

One of my colleagues began to lead this woman to Jesus. I took hold of the microphone and gave some instruction. "If you see people fall over, please don't be concerned. It's only God!" I felt I had to give them some sort of warning because of what was happening whenever we stepped out to pray like this. We would see people fall under the power of the Holy Spirit. If you want to know why we use chairs for HOTS, then this is one of the reasons!

No sooner had I spoken than the woman whom my colleague was leading to Jesus fell flat on her back onto the grass. It happened suddenly and without warning and took me by surprise. The crowd gasped. No one had touched her and no one had caught her! The woman got up off the ground and with excitement exclaimed that God had healed one of her eyes that had always been colour blind. Physically and spiritually she had gone from monochrome to Technicolor.

The crowd buzzed with excitement, the air full of God's electrifying presence. A man walked forward, his body riddled with arthritis and in constant pain. "Can God heal me?" he asked hopefully.

"Yes, he can," I replied, my faith on a high. As I touched his head he fell to the ground. You could hear what sounded like bones cracking as he lay in the grass. He rose to his feet, weeping and totally healed. His sister-in-law approached me next. She was already weeping and said, "I have the same condition as my brother-in-law." She too fell to the ground and stood up healed. At this point the crowd pressed in with many wanting prayer. I couldn't see any of our team.

"Christians, where are you?"

Have you ever seen an encouraged Christian? Faces like light bulbs and with the widest grins began popping up all over the crowd.

"Now start praying for everyone who needs healing and tell them about Jesus," I told them.

God has a sense of humour, if you didn't already know. The

man operating The Waltzer fairground ride thought he was in competition with us, because the crowd had joined us, and it was looking pretty lonely on his side. To draw attention he decided to turn the music up. I will never forget the track that came on as the team began to pray for people. It was by Queen: "Another one bites the dust, another one bites the dust, and another one's gone and another one's gone, another one bites the dust. Hey, hey I'm gonna get you too, another one bites the dust." All over the park bodies began to fall to the beat of the music! Many people were healed that day and opened their hearts to Jesus.

From a worldly perspective we might think a headache is easier to heal than a tumour on the brain. The degrees of difficulty go up in our mind and we've created a healing scale. What about schizophrenia or some incurable disease like diabetes? I am always amazed at Q&A time during our HOTS training seminars by the amount of people who ask the question, "Have you seen this, or that particular condition healed?"

What they are really saying, is, "This is my impossible mountain. I've never seen it moved by prayer." It's on the impossible end of their scale, but not from God's perspective.

We have a tendency to focus on the sickness and make an automatic assessment about the level of difficulty. On a scale of being "easy to heal" to "difficult, if not impossible" we'd rather pray for people on the easy end of our scale and try to avoid the "difficult, if not impossible" ones. And we haven't even started to talk about raising the dead!

Instead we should be focussing on Jesus and his all-encompassing victory over every sickness and disease. A major shift of perspective is called for. The cross dealt with every sickness and disease we are ever likely to encounter, even death. From the perspective of the cross there is no compartmentalisation or scale. Every sickness known to man has been dealt with and is now under the feet of Jesus.

"Surely he took up our infirmities and carried our sorrows" (Isaiah 53:4).

Isaiah's prophecy was fulfilled seven hundred and fifty years later, as Jesus the Lamb of God was nailed to the cross and became the perfect sacrifice, once for all time. "Surely" means "without doubt".

Jesus asked the question, "Which is easier: to say, 'Your sins are forgiven,' or to say, 'Get up and walk'?" (Matthew 9:5). The answer is neither and it doesn't matter, because Jesus has authority, all authority!

We don't have all the answers and we don't guarantee healing, although we know and believe that God has the power to heal. We want to give God all the honour, so we never accept any donations or money from people when we're on the streets. Rather we encourage people to let us know if they have been healed and to tell their family and friends what God has done for them – and to bring them along for prayer if they also need healing.

Whether they are healed or not, showing God's love is what makes the difference. No one who hasn't been healed has come back angry. On the contrary, they have been really touched that here are a group of people that genuinely care and even though they haven't been healed physically, their testimony is that God has made a difference in their lives. They experienced God's love and at the end of the day that's what really counts.

For the Christian there is always hope and faith in Jesus is not just for this life alone. Since Jesus has been raised from the dead, the believer can be assured of eternal life and know that, one day, all pain, suffering, tears and death will be wiped away forever.

12

DEVELOPING A HEALING ENVIRONMENT

I couldn't understand why some people were healed and some weren't, but when I look at my own journey from its Pentecostal beginnings into the Vineyard movement, there has been a progression in my understanding of how healing comes, which has shaped the development of the HOTS model, so that it becomes an environment in which the laity and ordinary believers can see the greatest number of people healed.

When I read the Scriptures, I see that Jesus took every sickness upon himself and suffered so that we wouldn't have to. Isaiah 53:4-5 says,

"Surely he took up our infirmities and carried our sorrows, yet we considered him stricken by God, smitten by him, and afflicted. But he was pierced for our transgressions, he was crushed for our iniquities; the punishment that brought us peace was upon him, and by his wounds we are healed."

As previously mentioned, the word "surely" here means "without a doubt". The Scripture assures us that Jesus died, not just for our sins, but for every sickness and disease there is, because he died for every condition known to mankind. Yet there is this dilemma in that our experience shows that not everyone is healed. This is the "now" and "not yet" of the kingdom of God.

Reading the Bible, we see Jesus and the disciples at times healing *all* the sick. There's no getting away from that. *All were healed.* So that includes people whose lives were completely messed up and people who were following other gods. In healing the multitudes Jesus made no distinctions whatsoever.

Matthew 8:16-17 says,

"When evening came, many who were demon-possessed were brought to him, and he drove out the spirits with a word and healed all the sick. This was to fulfil what was spoken through the prophet Isaiah: 'He took up our infirmities and carried our diseases.'"

Later on, in Matthew 12:15 we read:

"Many followed him, and he healed *all* their sick"

And again, in Matthew 14:35b-36:

"People brought all their sick to him and begged him to let the sick just touch the edge of his cloak, and *all who touched him were healed.*"

On many occasions everyone was healed, yet at the other end of the spectrum we see Jesus in his own home town where, "He could not do any miracles there, except lay his hands on a few sick people and heal them. And he was amazed at their lack of faith" (Mark 6:5-6).

It almost seems as if Jesus wanted to heal and was willing to heal, but wasn't able to because of their lack of faith.

When somebody's not healed, many have been damaged by the words that have been spoken to them by people who told them they just didn't have enough faith and they've put the onus on them. But what I see from the Scripture is there are just some environments so full of scepticism and unbelief as to create an atmosphere where God can't work, because the bottom line is that he needs people to believe. Some have gone overboard with the faith teaching, but there's no escaping the fact that Jesus talked about the need for faith.

Jesus said to the woman with the issue of blood, "Take heart, daughter, your faith has healed you" (Matthew 9:22). And to the friends of the paralytic: "When Jesus saw their faith, he said to the paralytic, 'Take heart, son; your sins are forgiven.'"

There has to be faith somewhere, whether in the person in need of healing, or their family or friends. My primary gifting is one of faith, and faith for healing is something that's been developing in my life right from the very beginning – it's not something that happened overnight. My faith and hunger to see healing was fuelled by reading the Bible and just wanting to be like Jesus.

As I've studied the Scriptures and read in Luke 5:17b that, "the power of the Lord was present for him to heal the sick," I've come to the conclusion that there has to be an environment where his presence and his power are there, and where people have faith and are believing in him. The HOTS model has developed into becoming just such an environment.

Jesus said, "The kingdom of God is within you" (Luke 17:21) so my understanding is that we're to bring his kingdom rule into every environment. We're to take back what has been robbed from us and we're to bring the rule and reign of the kingdom to earth: "Your kingdom come, your will be done on earth as it is in heaven" (Matthew 6:10).

We're tasked with creating an environment where Heaven is present on earth and where anything can happen.

I believe that if Jesus had had time to spend in his own home town, he would have turned the situation there around. Little by little, the atmosphere would have changed, because he talks about the kingdom being like light and yeast and salt. You cannot be light and yeast and salt in a place without affecting everything around you.

When we're doing HOTS we understand that we are a royal priesthood, carriers of divine presence. The Holy Spirit lives in us and we are to carry the atmosphere of Heaven everywhere. Wherever God's presence goes, the power, authority and rule of his kingdom is impressed upon this world. The manifestation of God's presence is a sign that God is alive and amongst his people. His tangible presence changes everything. We are awakening people to the reality of God through his Spirit.

In the Old Testament the Levites were the priests who carried the Ark of the Covenant which was the instrument through which God manifested his presence on earth. We're like the Levites in Joshua chapter 3 who stepped into the River Jordan in full flood to allow the Israelites to walk across on dry ground into all the promises of God.

The waters fled back as a sign and a wonder and began to head for outer space, so that everyone for miles around could see that God's people had arrived. Just as the Levite priests stepped into the impossible, so we must step with bold faith into the world to enable those outside of God's kingdom to encounter God's love and power, and meet with Jesus.

Our banner announces Healing and we stand on the streets and release everything that God's given to us, recognising who we are. We are temples of the Holy Spirit who lives within us, and out of our innermost being flows rivers of living water. We are the aroma of Christ wherever we go. We are the fragrance of life to those being saved or the smell of death to those who are perishing. Either way we should be seeing people running towards us or fleeing from us.

We are Christ's ambassadors, representing his kingdom, so whatever ground we stand on becomes the very place where we are representing him. Where we stand is where the kingdom of God is made manifest. An awareness and understanding of that brings a release of the kingdom. His presence breaks out when we recognise who we are and what it is we carry.

Without saying a word, just the very fact and conscious understanding of who it is that lives in us, who we represent, and the fact that we are seated in heavenly places with him, means that everything around us has to change. A conscious awareness of this will change our environment so that people can encounter the King and experience the kingdom; so that they can taste and see that God is good. In such an environment anything can happen as people encounter God – healing, deliverance and salvation.

When I got saved I walked into the presence of God. There is no escaping his presence as Psalm 139 so beautifully describes, so in my thinking it doesn't matter whether people sit in the chairs or not. HOTS isn't about getting bums on seats so we can say we prayed for x number of people today, rather it is the fact of changing the environment in your town and city by standing there and representing Jesus the King, releasing all he's given to you and all that you've received during the week.

Our preparation is our relationship with God, our intimacy

with him, and drawing from that deep well to create an oasis so that thirsty people passing by will be drawn. If there is a spiritual hunger in people and a thirst, and if there is living water where you are, they will be drawn to you.

I believe HOTS is creating an environment of faith where the church becomes visible and people can see something different. Simply by walking past they will experience the presence of God.

A colleague of one of our team members saw her praying for the sick when she was going through the town one Saturday. The following Monday at work she began to ask her questions:

"I saw you praying with that group of people outside the Town Hall on Saturday. I was compelled to stop and watch. I felt this strong presence and became very emotional. I walked as far back as I could until my back was against the wall of the bank. I could still sense this presence. Tell me, was that God?"

When we go out onto the streets, God's presence goes with us. We become the church without walls, where people who wouldn't normally walk into a church building can experience God. They don't have to come and sit on a chair for prayer to encounter him. Just by walking past they can experience God's presence and healing power.

In such environments we're going to see more and more healing taking place, physical, emotional and spiritual, because where the Spirit of the Lord is there is freedom. There are times where Heaven just opens on earth in an amazing way, and that's the grace of God.

Nevertheless, it's important to count the cost before starting HOTS in your community. Such a ministry is a long-term venture which requires commitment, perseverance and dogged determination.

"Because the Sovereign Lord helps me, I will not be disgraced" says the prophet Isaiah, "Therefore have I set my face like flint, and I know I will not be put to shame" (Isaiah 50:7).

If you set your face like flint and have faith that God is at work helping you, then all the various diversions, distractions and disappointments that the enemy will send to blow you off course will not succeed. There are bound to be quiet times and busy times, but you can be assured that God is always doing something. His work continues unseen long after you have packed up your equipment and left. The impact you make in your community and afar is enormous. You truly are the answer to the prayers of those who cry out for help to a God they do not know.

13

EQUIPPING THE SAINTS

Week after week we saw God doing the most amazing things on the streets and the incredible significance of what he was doing and where it might lead was just beginning to dawn upon us. One man who was wonderfully healed was Hugh from Strabane. In 2005 Hugh had been diagnosed with cancer of the prostate and he was in a lot of pain. The hospital had run all the tests and told him that his cancer was terminal, but his friends had told him about "God's workers" on the streets of Coleraine, so he came for prayer one Saturday in March 2007. As the team laid their hands on him and prayed, he experienced heat coming into his body and felt he had been cleared of the cancer.

A couple of months later, he went back to see his doctor. In order to get him seen quickly, and believing the cancer to be much worse by this stage, his doctor referred him to the hospital at Omagh. The specialists there ran all the usual tests and as Hugh watched them carefully studying the screen for a full ten minutes, he feared the worst. But instead, they turned to him and said they could find no trace of cancer in his body at all!

Hugh came back to tell us what had happened and because he also had a problem with pain in his arm, he thought that he may as well get prayer for that to be healed as well. The team laid their hands on his arm and again he felt God taking all the pain from him. He'd been a milkman for 53 years and could barely drive a lorry, having to change the gears with his opposite hand, yet he testified that the next day he was able to work wonders with that hand and was free of pain.

Returning to tell us this good news, Hugh then asked the team, "Can you get anyone off cigarettes?" He'd spent a lot of money trying to quit smoking, but later told us that after prayer that Saturday he'd never given cigarettes another thought, nor had he experienced any craving.

By now we were also seeing a lot of people coming to faith and news of what was happening in our community began to spread. The main stories that caught people's imagination and fuelled interest in what we were doing were Hugh's story and the healing of the woman in the wheelchair from Cavan.

When other church leaders began to hear about what was happening in Coleraine, they came to visit us to see what God was doing on the streets. One such leader was David McClay, a Church of Ireland rector in inner-city Belfast. For four years David had been the rector at Willowfield, where he had engaged in every type of evangelism possible in an effort to connect with those outside the church.

All the time their outreach was changing the atmosphere in their community and people's perception about the church and what Christians were like, but David's frustration was that he wasn't seeing a lot in the way of people being healed or coming to faith in Christ. He longed to see God moving in power in Belfast and to see his own people exercising all the gifts of the Spirit beyond the church's walls.

Having seen the HOTS model in action, David invited me to Willowfield to train a team to take HOTS out onto the streets of Belfast. The beauty of HOTS is that it's reproducible, transferable and sustainable, and people can access it really quickly. David's congregation caught the HOTS model straight away and used it to reach out to the people in their community with immediate and encouraging results.

Every Saturday morning people turned up to be prayed for, and David began to see a lot more in the way of healing and people coming to faith. As David headed up the New Wine network of churches in Ireland, and he began sharing stories of what they were experiencing among those churches, many started asking how they also could access the training and the HOTS model.

As interest was rapidly increasing, David and I made a recording for the New Wine "Leadership for Life" series, explaining the model and giving testimonies. This went out to every church in the New Wine network and catapulted HOTS from something that was incredibly local at that point to something interdenominational, because New Wine's reach included Baptist and Anglican, as well as other church movements.

Over the following months as the invitations came in, I was travelling all over the UK to train church teams. As the ministry began to grow and flourish, my schedule became increasingly full and there were many occasions where churches were having to wait several months to be trained. I was away from home most weekends and although my energy levels were holding up, and Linda and the boys were amazingly supportive, I realised what it was costing them. It was imperative to find a way to train others that didn't crush either me or my family.

Whilst HOTS began as a ministry within the local church, its exponential growth signified that God was up to something much greater than one location or denomination. The New Wine churches had embraced HOTS incredibly well, but at a New Wine conference in Harrogate in May of 2008 a healing happened which exposed the model more widely among the traditional denominations.

Frances Finn's left leg was one and a half inches shorter than the right one. She was the presenter of BBC Radio Nottingham's mid-morning show, and as I prayed for her, and her leg grew out so that both were the same length, someone filmed it on their mobile phone and posted it on YouTube.

Frances subsequently spoke about her healing on her radio programme and the publicity this generated meant that Catholic churches, United Reformed churches, Methodist churches and even churches who didn't doctrinally believe in healing now started getting involved!

About this time some articles began appearing in the Christian press linking HOTS with church unity and revival, and while it was exciting to see different streams of churches working together, what was most thrilling for me was that more and more Christians were out on the streets sharing their faith and praying for healing, making Jesus known in towns and cities across the nation. This is what HOTS is primarily about – moving the Church beyond the building onto the streets using the vehicle of healing.

Until this point much of HOTS happened centrally, processed

and directed by the Causeway Coast Vineyard church. It was our desire and, we felt, our kingdom responsibility to continue the expansion of HOTS and to equip local churches to engage with the community beyond their walls, so we felt it less than ideal that many churches were now having to wait several months to be trained. Our initial way of resolving this was to increase the training materials, producing CDs and DVDs, and making these freely available to any church requesting them.

However, the more accessible the training became, and the more the resources were made available, the greater the demand was for help and support in launching HOTS. Each training event I did created the need for more training events, as oftentimes many other churches were represented at the local church training weekends, and once they heard the model explained and saw it demonstrated, they also expressed a desire to be trained.

Each week, churches and church leaders both in the UK and now from further afield were contacting us to find out about how to lead their people out onto the streets, so that by 2010 HOTS had expanded to 700 churches in seventeen countries! It was obvious that the future of HOTS required a more decentralised approach, but the challenge for us was how to encourage and facilitate all this expansion whilst safeguarding against the dilution of the model.

Furthermore, simply providing churches with the training materials had its limitations, in that the CDs and DVDs could only explain the model, they couldn't demonstrate it. Whilst the model can be replicated fairly simply, it's only a shell unless filled with the same passion and perspective that gave birth to the original. Some things are more caught than taught. The aspects of HOTS that cannot be gleaned from following the manual are best experienced directly from those who carry the presence of God and his authority and are able to impart it to others.

The Causeway Coast Vineyard's goal throughout was to serve the local church and enable the local church to fulfil its missional calling, so it was important for us to train as many people as possible from the local church. To that end, the Causeway Coast Vineyard launched a series of conferences in 2010 which we called The Church has left the Building. We hosted these conferences in various cities throughout the UK to train groups of churches simultaneously, whilst at the same time enabling churches to explore the ethos of HOTS in an accessible venue and at an affordable cost.

Together with this training initiative, and recognising the need to develop the leadership of HOTS, we also began the process of identifying and releasing regional trainers. These were to be people who were submitted to their local church and who we recognised could be trusted to faithfully steward the direction, vision and influence of HOTS, and provide governance for the model in a way that retained its core identity, whilst at the same time releasing its influence among other churches. These regional HOTSpots as we called them, would also allow us to better respond to other communities and countries outside the UK.

As we rethought the training and leadership, we also had to rethink the infrastructure, because up until this point all the resources and assistance to churches wanting to launch HOTS in their community had been provided for free, with the cost borne solely by the Causeway Coast Vineyard (in 2010 we estimated the annual cost to be in the region of £65,000) and a quarter of our church staff were focussed entirely on helping other churches launch and adapt the model to their context.

We took the decision to set up a HOTS partnership whereby partner churches would receive free training CDs and DVDs, downloadable training manuals, templates and sample letters, together with regular newsletters, discounted rates on banners, and some other benefits, in addition to connection and networking with other churches for support and to share stories.

As HOTS continued to expand into new communities and new countries the Causeway Coast Vineyard was faced with several challenges: how its growth and development could be funded, how to assist existing partners, and how to ensure the integrity of the model wasn't compromised. I was also personally facing a challenge from the Lord to step out more and more into the impossible and to move out beyond what I was comfortable with to pray for conditions I'd never seen healed before.

Normally when I visit churches, the training runs over a Friday evening and a Saturday morning and when I come to the end of the training, in order to demonstrate the model, I pray for one or two people. One of the things I often do is to pray for legs to lengthen. So I invite people to come up and sit on a chair if they have any problem with their legs or back, or if they know they have one leg shorter than the other.

The reason I do this is because it's so visible. It accelerates people to a place of either faith or unbelief. When someone's leg grows out it fast-tracks a person's faith to expose what's in their heart, because sometimes the heart needs to be challenged by seeing with the eyes something that is really mind-blowing.

On one particular occasion when I was in Watford, a lady came and sat on the chair and I demonstrated the HOTS model with this lady and her leg grew out. I then asked whether there was anyone else with a similar problem who'd also like prayer. Another lady, Heather, came forward and explained that her foot turned inwards whenever she walked, and two weeks previously her doctor had diagnosed that her problem with walking was due to the fact that one leg was shorter than the other. She sat on the chair and I got the lady who'd just been healed to pray for her and her leg grew out. When she went to test it she found she could walk perfectly and her foot had stopped turning in!

A little while later I received a follow-up email filling me in on the rest of the story. Heather believed God had healed her but she wanted to be 100% sure this had happened, so she went to her doctor to get checked over to verify her healing. She was wondering how she was going to explain to him what had happened in case he'd think she was crazy, when she noticed a verse of Scripture on display in his surgery. Realising he might be a believer, she began by telling him that she was a Christian and went to church. When he told her she was speaking to the converted, she was encouraged to relate exactly what had happened.

His response was, "Well, there are these anomalies that happen, but as a doctor I must examine you thoroughly."

When he had finished his examination and taken several detailed measurements, including putting a spirit level to her hips, he said to her,

"I can't say exactly where, but somewhere, bone has grown and it's perfect now."

The miracle of God lengthening legs by growing bone is astonishing and I love demonstrating healing by praying for legs to lengthen, but it had become safe for me and there was no growth in it for me personally. Also I'd reached a point where I had so much expectation for legs to grow that when I was demonstrating healing, wanting as many people to see it as possible, I would wait for everyone to gather round and then lift the legs up and measure them very quickly and put them back down on the ground, because if I held onto them for too long they would just grow in my hand and then I wouldn't be able to show anybody. That might sound arrogant, but it's actually my gift of faith that is constant and healing comes with that.

So wanting to be stretched in my own faith, I said at one of The Church has left the Building conferences, "Today I want to pray for something I've never seen happen before, to see something healed that I've never seen healed before."

People were calling out all manner of conditions:

"Kneecaps forming."

"No," I said, "I've seen that happen."

"Blindness?"

"No, I've seen blind eyes opened."

Then somebody shouted out, "But I have no eye!"

"Okay, that'll do!" I said, "I've never yet seen an eyeball form."

Everyone gathered round and we began praying. The faith level in the room was such that we were more amazed that the person didn't receive a brand new eyeball than if they had.

Far from being disappointed, this only spurred me on to reach for more. I have had the privilege of seeing God do some wonderful and astounding things, but I am not content to settle for anything less than the "more" God has for me.

Jesus promised in John 14:12 that, "...anyone who has faith in me will do what I have been doing. He will do even greater things than these, because I am going to the Father."

Jesus has promised that I would do greater things in both quantity and quality than he did, so I am pressing on to take hold of that for which Jesus Christ has taken hold of me.

14

THE BELIEVER'S AUTHORITY

There are many models for healing and it would be a mistake to get too caught up in the HOTS model per se without fully appreciating the need to understand not just the role and importance of faith, but also the authority that is resident in the believer.

From my reading of the Scriptures, it's pretty clear to me that Jesus is always our role model, so when I read in Acts 10:38, "how God anointed Jesus of Nazareth with the Holy Spirit and power, and how he went around doing good and healing all who were under the power of the devil, because God was with him," my understanding is that wherever Jesus went he was demonstrating total liberation out of his relationship of intimacy with the Father. Jesus modelled a creative, fluid lifestyle of healing based on his close relationship with the Father, and his absolute authority over every demon, sickness and disease.

Obviously though, he had a goal and a strategy, because in Luke 4:43 he told the crowds that were following him, "I must preach the good news of the kingdom of God to the other towns also, because that is why I was sent."

The problem for Jesus was that he ministered very publicly. He healed the sick openly in full view of everyone, and when people saw the things that he did they followed him, they put their faith in him, and they praised the God of Israel.

Jesus did things very openly so people would believe in God, but ministering in such a way actually became a hindrance to him, because he could only do so much. In laying aside his majesty, he was showing the world what one man in communion with the Father could do. Yet he was also showing the limitations of the one-man ministry, recognising that he couldn't do everything himself. So in Luke 10:2 he tells the disciples, "The harvest is plentiful, but the workers are few. Ask the Lord of the harvest, therefore, to send out workers into his harvest field."

Jesus' strategy for the harvest was to equip the disciples who'd been following him and watching the way he ministered. He called them to him and gave them authority to heal every sickness, to cleanse those with skin conditions, to raise the dead and drive out demons, and to tell people wherever they went that the kingdom of God was close at hand.

But Jesus didn't stop at the Twelve and make them superstars or celebrity figures. He gave the very same authority to seventy-two others also and he sent them out. Luke 10:17 says: "The seventy-two returned with joy and said, 'Lord, even the demons submit to us in your name.'"

The reason they were filled with joy wasn't because of any technique or model they'd used, but the fact that they'd been given authority, that authority had worked, and they could hardly believe what they were seeing.

Jesus was also filled with joy because they'd understood it.

"I saw Satan fall like lightning from heaven. I have given you authority to trample on snakes and scorpions and to overcome all the power of the enemy; nothing will harm you." (Luke 10:18)

He'd given them authority, they'd exercised that authority and they'd seen that it worked.

But Jesus didn't stop there. He then gave the Great Commission to all believers:

"All authority in heaven and on earth has been given to me. Therefore go and make disciples of all nations, baptising them in the name of the Father and of the Son and of the Holy Spirit, and teaching them to obey everything I have commanded you." (Matthew 28:18-20)

In other words, "Heal the sick, raise the dead, cleanse those who have leprosy, drive out demons. Freely you have received, freely give." (Matthew 10:8)

This is the master plan that the Lord had of making disciples to do the things that he did. Jesus didn't say "Bring everyone to me." In fact, when he delivered the Gadarene man, instead of letting him follow him, he told him to go home and tell his family everything that God had done for him and the man went back and evangelised the whole area (Mark 5:19-20).

What I see Jesus doing is showing us what God can do and telling us to now go and do likewise – to go and share this good news with our family, friends and neighbours. Healing was never meant to be confined to a building, one model, or ministered through just a few. It was meant to happen naturally anywhere, everywhere and at any time, through every believer to everyone!

Jesus wanted the disciples to exercise the authority they had in any and every situation. I believe that even when he was having a power nap in the fishing boat and the storm came up, he was hoping they'd at least have a go at using their authority instead of being so fearful – and all the time he's trying to instil faith in them and teach them not to doubt.

He knows they're going to find it hard to believe, because it's not yet within their perspective. It flies in the face of their natural senses. But Jesus is constantly teaching them and gradually, over three years, we see this progression from disciples who are terrified to disciples who are confident. We see them moving from a place of fear to a place of faith.

It's the same for us. The Holy Spirit will give us the right perspective and we'll learn, and as we learn, if we hold on to Jesus' teaching so that we are truly his disciples, then we'll know the truth, and the truth will set us free to be able to do the things Jesus did. But we have to be obedient and hold onto his teaching, even when it doesn't make sense, even when it looks foolish and flies in the face of what this world says.

For forty days after the resurrection Jesus talked to his disciples about the kingdom of God till they'd finally grasped it, they were free, they'd come to the place where Peter could say to a crippled beggar, "Silver or gold I do not have, but what I have I give you. In the name of Jesus Christ of Nazareth, walk" (Acts 3:6).

The Lord wants the Church to know what it is we've been given. He wants us to know the authority we have, our position in Christ, what it is we carry, and who it is that we represent.

The mind of Christ, the heart of the Father, and the life of the Spirit in a believer changes the status quo. Believers make a difference wherever they go and the enemy will do everything he can to stop the Church from knowing and walking in its God-given authority, because all of Heaven will break loose otherwise.

Jesus has given us the keys of the kingdom which represent his authority. Whenever we exercise that authority on earth, all of Heaven backs it up. But we have to be childlike in our faith to see the Kingdom of God and we have to believe what Jesus says, because some of the things Jesus says sound so crazy that only a child could possibly believe it. It's like a dad might say to his son, "Son, if you do this, you can fly," and the son's eyes fill with wonder and he believes he can fly because his father says so. He doesn't even question it and even though he might try to fly and fail, he still doesn't question it because he believes his dad.

I emphasise authority particularly, because a lot of the time Christians can be so wishy-washy with the way that they pray. The words that come from our mouths can betray what we actually believe or understand. Wherever I go, I teach about authority because if the Church gets the revelation and gets holds of the understanding of this, no sickness or demon will be able to stand in the way of it; nothing will be impossible.

An illustration of the authority we have in Jesus happened on the memorable return journey of a combined training trip to a church in Slovakia with Alan, Kathryn, myself and a team. We taught on leadership, worship and HOTS. After an amazing time there, seeing the church inspired and activated, we left our hotel around 3am in the morning to make the arduous three-hour long journey to Bratislava airport to catch our flight home.

The car I travelled in was cramped and uncomfortable and it was impossible for me to sleep on the way to the airport. I was so tired on arriving at the airport that I could have fallen asleep standing up in the queue to check in our luggage. All I could dream about was getting a window seat on our plane and the promise of blissful sleep!

Alan, who is always full of creative and bright ideas, came up with a plan. When we first flew in to Slovakia, and on landing in Bratislava, we had to get a bus from our plane to the terminal. He reasoned that for our flight home, if we were last in the queue in the departure lounge we would be first off the bus that would take us to our plane, which meant we could have the pick of the seats. Logically, this sounded like music to my weary brain, as anyone who knows me and knows how I like to travel knows I would do almost anything to get a window seat!

To my dismay, as the gates opened for us to board we saw our plane conveniently parked outside. Being last in the queue meant we were last on the plane. As we boarded I glanced down the aisle and could see all the window seats were taken, but five rows down the front of the plane I saw a free aisle seat. It was next to a slim Spanish woman who sat in the middle seat with her boyfriend, who had the window seat. I thought because she was so slim I would have elbow room to my left, and the aisle meant I had elbow room to my right.

As I buckled up I wasn't even going to listen to the safety demonstration, I was so tired. I bowed my head to sleep. It would only have taken 30 seconds, but then this Spanish lady sitting next to me announced, "Excuse me, I suffer with a severe fear of flying and I make everyone nervous around me. If you wish to get some rest on this flight could I please suggest you go to the back of the plane?"

I was feeling pretty grumpy and thought to myself, "There's no way I'm moving from this seat. If anything is moving it's going to be her fear!"

I turned to her and smiled as best I could and replied, "Don't worry; my peace will balance out your fear."

She gave me an odd look wondering what on earth I meant, but then as the plane began to take off, true to her word this lady began to panic.

"What's that noise?" she said frantically, her poor boyfriend trying to explain to her that the engine wasn't about to fall off the wing. He did his best to allay her fears, which unfortunately only compounded the situation and made it worse. He realised he wasn't helping and decided the best thing he could do was totally ignore her and superglue his nose to the window.

Things were getting out of hand and I thought I had better do something. I looked behind me to see if there were any team members nearby for support. I spotted Stephen five rows behind me. He was already asleep. "Typical!" I murmured. Alan, Kathryn and the rest of the team were further back and blissfully unaware of the drama unfolding in row five. I looked across the aisle and saw a man opposite me reading a book. After looking at him for a moment I thought to myself, "He looks like a Christian."

I slowly began to lean across the aisle and stretched my neck to try and see what book he was reading. When I had reached a 45-degree angle across the aisle, almost falling out of my seat (anyone sitting behind must have been wondering what on earth I was up to) I could see that this man was indeed reading a Christian book. It turned out that he was part of a ministry that for years had imported Bibles into Eastern Europe.

I turned to him asking, "Excuse me, you look like a Christian, do you follow Jesus?" He looked surprised and acknowledged that he was a Christian but must have been wondering what I was going to say next. "The lady sitting next to me has this fear of flying and I'm about to drive the fear out of her. Could you please quietly support me in prayer while I do that?"

The look of concern that flashed across his face didn't escape me as he agreed to something he most probably thought shouldn't happen on a plane. I turned to the Spanish woman and said, "I follow Jesus and I believe he can help you be completely free from your fear. Could I please pray for you?"

"Yes, please!" she replied without hesitation.

I turned to her boyfriend, his nose still stuck to the window.

"Excuse me, I hope you don't mind if I pray for your girlfriend, I believe Jesus can remove her fear."

I didn't want him to think I was making a pass at his girlfriend.

"Yes! Yes please!" he replied.

I think he would have agreed to anything at that point. I swivelled in my seat towards the woman, turning my back to the aisle and I took hold of her wrist. I didn't want to bring attention to what I was doing, so I began to pray quietly, but firmly,

"Fear, I command you to come out of this woman and never return!"

The spirit of fear came out of her with a shriek, causing everyone in the first five rows to jump in their seats and turn around. Stephen, five rows back, woke up with a start. Two air stewardesses came and stood behind me, asking if everything was okay, but I ignored them, being determined not to be diverted from my prayer for this woman until I knew she was completely free.

Suddenly she exclaimed, "It's gone, it's gone, my fear is gone!"

She started looking for her fear but it was nowhere to be seen. Her boyfriend was speechless. Not knowing how to thank me she rummaged around in her handbag and pulled out a pen and gave it to me.

"It's a pen," I thought. "I've always wanted one of these."

Then receiving some inspiration I said to her: "This pen represents your fear, and you've given it to Jesus. Whenever you're afraid you can always talk to him."

I was able to swap seats with Maxine, another team member, so that Maxine could chat and pray with her. Then later on I talked to her about what a relationship with Jesus was like and explained that prayer was simply talking with Jesus. I saw her bow her head as she began to talk with Jesus. I never did get to sleep for the rest of the flight. Instead I quietly lifted her up to Jesus in prayer.

2 Timothy 4:2 says, "Preach the Word; be prepared in season and out of season."

We need to be ready to pray with anyone, at any time and in any place, whether it's convenient or inconvenient.

People often ask me how they can pray with greater authority. The answer is not to pray for more authority, but to ask the Holy Spirit to give you more revelation of the authority you have already been delegated.

When we pray for healing out on the streets, the distinguishing features of the HOTS model are the two particular ways we minister healing to people: by the laying on of hands and by the word of command. The touch part is the compassion and the love of God, but the word of command is an actual, intentional directing of one's prayer to move a mountain. In actual fact, those who truly understand they have authority don't have to command anything, because everything they do is authoritative. They know it, and the devil knows they know it. They could say "rhubarb" and still be exercising authority.

We've all heard about men and women of God who've had

amazing ministries and they have been gifts to the Church, but by and large these are people to whom authority comes naturally. Whether they've been consciously aware of it or not, it's obvious that they carry authority just by the way they pray and the way they behave.

The problem with authority comes when it is abused or misused. There's been a lack of wisdom in the use of authority sometimes so that, for example, when someone who is incredibly gifted prays from the platform in front of many watching people and they're successfully seeing people healed, there seems to be a natural drawing of people to want to go to that person for prayer, or to want that person to pray for everybody.

The problem is compounded if they continually minister by themselves and fail to teach the Church that they have been given authority to do that and show them how to do it. This is not what Jesus modelled. In the feeding of the four and five thousand, Jesus says to his disciples, "You feed them." He wants to hand it to others to do. He encourages them to take a risk and give whatever they have to God, and then he demonstrates the amazing things that can happen when something is given to God and then released.

Further problems arise from the one-man ministry when that person chooses to exercise their authority unwisely, theatrically, or in a way that is not relevant to, or in conflict with the culture they're in. People see the miracles and think that's amazing, but it's counter-productive if someone comes away thinking, "Well, that's the person of power for the hour, but there's no way I could do that in my office. There are some sick people where I work, but there's no way I could pray for them in that way. I'd probably get the sack."

That kind of wrong thinking and wrong perspective comes from seeing someone ministering very publicly and choosing to release healing in a way that has not been helpful, either by hitting someone or doing something that's off-the-wall.

My aim is to try and reverse that, to show the Church that it is the work of the Church, because the Scripture says believers, "...will place their hands on sick people and they will get well" (Mark 16:18).

Placing your hand on someone, touching them gently, is one of the most compassionate things you can do, because touch can convey so much. It was the way that Jesus modelled ministry.

"Filled with compassion, Jesus reached out his hand and touched the man." (Mark 1:41)

In London when we launched HOTS, a man came and he was watching us pray and then he walked away as if to go, but came back again. He did this two or three times and then he came over to me and said,

"This is so good – touch. We've lost this in our community and what I'm seeing here is one human being touching another gently and compassionately. This is what we need. This is the way of healing for our community."

The enemy has sought to abuse touch to rob us of that. That man could see that touch is something we've lost, so one of the things I'm wanting to regain is what it means to lay on hands. Laying on of hands sounds a little cold, but touch communicates so much.

When my three sons were born I would hug and kiss them all the time. As they got bigger I still hugged them, but when they started playing rugby and they were bigger than me, it wasn't so cool to do that, because I didn't want to embarrass them. But I could still convey so much by putting my hand on their shoulder. With a touch I could say, "I love you to bits. I'm proud of you. It's okay, I understand. Don't worry. Don't be afraid. You're safe."

All these things can be communicated through touch and we need to regain the art of touching appropriately and what this means, instead of using our hands for violence, to manipulate or to exert control. So when I see someone do something abusive in ministry, I know that's not of God. Even if they say God told them to do it and that person's healed, and they might think the end justifies the means, my response is that God will heal because he gives us authority to heal the sick, but what he doesn't do, is tell us how to use it.

How we decide to minister healing is entirely our choice. We may have the idea of doing it in any number of ways, but the fact is we have authority and we can abuse and misuse it through misunderstanding or a lack of wisdom. I've proven this by ministering in so many different ways.

When I was teaching a group of ten- and eleven-year-olds at New Wine how to pray, I had a word of knowledge for skin conditions, and while I was wondering how to give this word, a boy shouted out, "Can God do anything about eczema?"

Taking that as my cue, I said, "If you have eczema, stand up."

I didn't realise how common the condition was, because so many young people stood up, but I got those who stood up to place their hand on the area where they had the condition and then asked those sitting around them to stand and lay their hands gently on them. I then began to explain how healing comes, either instantly, gradually, or with no sign of healing. I emphasised the latter because up to that point I'd never seen skin conditions healed instantly. I thought if these young people didn't see it happen instantly their faith might take a knock and I wanted them to understand that God is still at work and that he still loves them, even though they might not see any change. I explained that their healing can come as they go, gradually or the next day.

I then began to instruct them how to pray by speaking to the condition as though they were speaking to a mountain and commanding the mountain to move by saying, "Skin condition, go in the name of Jesus."

There was anything between five and six hundred young people in that meeting and as they were praying I could hear pockets of excitement breaking out all over the place. After a few minutes, I asked them to check their bodies out and when I asked, "Who's been healed?" lots of hands went up.

My heart was challenged because of their youthful exuberance, but one of the leaders came up to me and said miracles were happening all over. A ten-year-old girl had eczema on the inside of her elbow and arm so bad she couldn't even touch her own body and no-one else could lay hands on her because of the pain. Yet, as they prayed they watched the eczema disappear before their eyes! The kingdom of God just broke out everywhere; these young people saw miracles taking place and they left there so impacted that days later parents were coming up to me asking what I'd done to their children. One young boy had chased a man on crutches and prayed for him there and then. The next day the parents saw the man without his crutches!

A couple of days later I was teaching an adult seminar, but a lot of these young people came in. I'd earlier spotted a water pistol, so I decided I would use that to demonstrate healing and authority. Noticing a few cheeky-looking boys, I said,

"I'm going to minister healing to you in the name of Jesus" and I squirted them and others who stood for healing a few times with the water pistol. Later, when I asked who'd been healed, hands went up and parents stood to confirm that their children had been healed. I did the same thing the following year with an AirZooka. That toy shoots out a harmless ball of air from a distance of up to forty feet, and from that distance I ministered healing to those who stood, before I gave the toy to one delighted little boy who'd been healed!

Problems arise when people focus on the method by which healing comes, rather than by the exercise of the authority that lies behind it. So I want to emphasise not the method, but the understanding that when you have authority you can choose the way you release that authority.

Doctors often come to me and ask how they can pray for patients in their surgery without laying hands on them. Christian doctors are in a perfect position, sometimes more directly than I am, because they already have the heart of God to heal the sick.

I tell them that what they need is a "faith hook", something that will help them release the power of God in a way of their own choosing. Laying on of hands is only one way. When I lay hands on someone I'm believing that in that moment of contact, the power of God is being released to heal that person. But there are many ways to establish a contact point with the Holy Spirit. In Acts 19:11-12, we read that,

"God did extraordinary miracles through Paul, so that even handkerchiefs and aprons that had touched him were taken to the sick, and their illnesses were cured and the evil spirits left them."

So for one doctor I know, the moment she takes the pulse

of a patient is the moment she consciously chooses to release healing to that person. Another doctor I know chooses to release healing the moment he puts the written prescription into his patient's hand.

When we understand just who we are, we also understand that whatever we touch is transformed and changed because of who we are and what we carry. I believe the kingdom of God is being released with healing and signs and wonders through many Christians who are completely ignorant of the fact. How much more would we be seeing if the Church fully understood the power and authority invested in it!

15

ROOTED IN THE LOCAL CHURCH

We are to affect our community wherever God has placed us, but in order to do that Christians in that community have to have a way of connecting with each other. This is the place of the local church. We gather to worship God and to hear from him; to be equipped and to receive his direction for the community we live in. The church exists for those outside of its walls, so we gather to scatter.

God gives a strategy for reaching every community through the local church and because we're interdependent, we're like a body needing all its parts to function. We're all connected to each other; no one is indispensible and God's plan is that we step out together into the hurting, broken places of this world with a clear vision of what he wants us to do.

Accordingly, it's vital that we don't give up meeting together. We need relationship; we need to be able to encourage, support and strengthen each other, and that comes from spending time together, breaking bread and simply doing life together. We're stronger and more effective together than we are apart.

Before the Israelites crossed over into the Promised Land they had a "Gilgal" – a base camp where they came together to remember all the things God had done and to praise him. In that gathered place they were restored and healed and directed by God to go out from there. There was a clear strategy. They heard from God what he wanted them to do and they went out and were successful. But we also see that when they went out and did their own thing, they failed spectacularly.

Meeting together as a church we gain strength when we sense God's presence. We're re-fuelled and re-focussed. It is vital to be rooted in the local church so that we can be healed from life's hurts, made whole and equipped and released with a clear vision and purpose.

So we are called to do things together and never apart, but there are obviously parts of the body that get more exposure than other parts, especially people in certain kinds of high-visibility ministry. Yet the reality is, they're no more important than someone who hides away and prays because that's what they've been called to do. A ministry that is unseen is no less important than one that is.

An evangelist in a high-visibility ministry like myself could be someone who's not completely submitted and committed to the God-given vision of the local church, and that person can then become dangerous and threatening to the leadership of the church. Furthermore, if that ministry begins to grow and separates from the local church, it then becomes a monster and does more harm than good.

My ministry is to do the work of an evangelist but also to equip the Church, and I'm called to do that where I live. God has called me to be a model for the Causeway Coast Vineyard and I'm wanting to model something where I totally submit myself to the leadership and the vision of the church. Alan Scott and I have an authentic and genuine relationship of complete trust, and that is so needed in church life. Every year we meet to affirm our deep affection for one another. I submit myself to his leadership and Alan likewise submits to what God's put into me.

I recognise that I am part of what God is doing in this community which is so precious to the Lord that he's put his church there. If I'm diverted from that, then I'm dishonouring what God's doing amongst us. Inevitably my travelling schedule means I'm away from the church a lot of the time, but I still belong to a small group and whether I'm at home or away, I always seek to honour the leadership and the church body. This is why I believe God is able to bless the ministry and expand it.

When we launched HOTS, Alan and I had an inkling of the journey that was in store for us. We often breakfasted together and dreamt about God visiting our community and declared God's divine destiny over each of our lives. Even though we had a sense back then that God was going to do something extraordinary in Coleraine that would go further into the nations, we are still in awe of his generosity, his mercy, his faithfulness and redemptive power.

In living the dream, we vowed to keep our feet on the ground and never lose sight of Jesus. Our part is to follow him and live as sons. Alan and Kathryn Scott's wise and humble leadership has created a safe place for me and many others to explore our divine destiny with the freedom to be creative and true to who God has made us to be. Their vision and example is enabling the culture of the kingdom to impact every aspect of community life.

Very early on when HOTS was still in its infancy, God had spoken very strongly to Alan to say that he was to protect the identity of HOTS and in particular its connection to the local church. HOTS was birthed in the local church and it was for the local church. The Holy Spirit clearly directed him to follow the model for ministry outlined in Acts 13:1-3:

"In the church at Antioch there were prophets and teachers ... While they were worshipping the Lord and fasting the Holy Spirit said, 'Set apart for me Barnabas and Saul for the work to which I have called them.' So after they had fasted and prayed, they placed their hands on them and sent them off."

Here we see a trans-local ministry which is birthed in a local church context and carried by those uniquely anointed, who are then released and commissioned for that particular task (by the local church) whilst continuing to function as part of a local church. The Scripture is clear that Paul and Barnabas, whilst having a mandate for the nations, still remained submitted to local church authority.

Because the mandate and the HOTS model were sovereignly initiated, we had to develop it so that it remained firmly within the local church. HOTS has never been about appointing and releasing itinerant individuals, but about equipping the Church for works of service to the lost and the least, so that the body of Christ may be built up.

HOTS is not an extension, an add-on, or just another church programme, but rather a core expression of our commitment to lost people. HOTS should be one seamless facet of a healthy, outward-looking church. That means the church lives and breathes reaching the lost and prunes anything that gets in the way of that.

The Causeway Coast Vineyard and HOTS are in partnership to do whatever is needed to help people come to Christ and we promote HOTS as part of our overall strategy of reaching lost people. HOTS has become an integral part of the life of the whole church and because we are always seeking ways to catalyse more people into this ministry, all our small groups have been trained in using the model.

The scale and reach of HOTS is truly incredible. Beginning with the European and Scandinavian nations, it's gone viral around the world because it's so immediately accessible and transferable, to the extent that HOTS teams can now be found on all five continents.

I confess to being as surprised as anyone at what has happened. When I led that first team out onto the streets of Coleraine, I could never have imagined in my wildest dreams that God would do even a fraction of what he has done in helping churches around the world to come together and step out of their buildings to see their communities transformed by the power of the gospel of Jesus Christ.

There are so many stories that could be told, but one that has especially touched my heart concerns William, who came to Warwick in England on a church placement from Uganda. This young man came to faith when he was living on the streets of Kampala with his younger sister. Together they fled the genocide in Rwanda when William was just nine years old, having witnessed the horrific murder of their parents.

The weekend William arrived, the churches in Warwick were out on the streets doing HOTS and he came along. Two of his toes were bent up and broken from a recent car accident, so that he was unable to wear shoes. As he sat in the chair, the bent toe straightened out and the adjacent curved toe lay flat. When he stood up and walked around, William found to his delight that all pain had gone. He was able to wear shoes to church the next day and vowed to set up a HOTS team on his return to Uganda.

At the end of his placement he returned home armed with the HOTS training DVDs and four dozen people immediately signed up to form three teams. These people were all from different churches and it was the first time the churches there had ever worked in partnership together. From day one they saw dozens of people coming to faith and experiencing healing in their bodies. Within seven months HOTS had spread to another twelve towns in that nation.

William's story of life as a street child prompted the family he'd stayed with in Warwick to fund a Christmas party for the local street children in Kampala. At that party 120 street children and vulnerable adults received Jesus and they in turn then began to go out to minister with the church teams at HOTS.

The following Easter they funded an even bigger party which attracted the attention of a Ugandan TV station. William's sister had formed the street children into a choir and they sang at the party to show the nation how God was using the Church to transform the lives of the street children.

Before long over 500 children were off the streets and more and more people were coming to faith, so that within a matter of months the churches were dealing with an influx of 1,000 new believers!

It was my privilege to meet William on a visit to England and lay hands on him to commission him to minister and grow HOTS right across his country and beyond. My prayer for him was, "What I have I give to you" and it was a joy to hear that within

18 months HOTS was flourishing in such a way that it had spread throughout the whole nation of Uganda, and on 31 December 2013 the HOTS teams held a celebration in Nakuvvubo Stadium for a gathering of thousands to pray in the New Year!

William's story is a book in itself. It is the most wonderful illustration of how God has used HOTS, not just to heal sick bodies, but to supernaturally intervene in the lives of the poor and orphaned, the rejected and marginalised to transform a nation.

What's most remarkable, perhaps, is that it's not the ministers who are leading this, it's the ordinary, incredible, exceptional people whose only goal is to make Jesus famous. Those whose lives echo the words of the prophet Isaiah when he says,

"Your name and your renown are the desire of our hearts." (Isaiah 26:8-9)

Something special happens when we begin to share Jesus and talk to people about him. An increasing hunger develops in us for God. It is easy for Christians to become jaded and lose their passion for God, to somehow stop sharing their faith and stop looking towards the lost. When we get involved with church programmes that are not outward focussed, they begin to sap our time and energy and before we know it, we've lost our zeal.

As much as anything, beyond my own involvement in pioneering and developing HOTS, and beyond people being healed, I am excited that in shopping centres, town squares, high streets, parks, farmers' markets and psychic fairs all over the UK (and now in a multitude of different locations across the world) you can find ordinary people across the denominations whose lives have been utterly transformed and who have been emboldened to step out of their buildings to reach their communities. Not with wise and persuasive words, but with a demonstration of the Holy Spirit's power.

So we care for our community in every way and everyone gets to play. Supernatural solutions for our cities require that we don't think "out of the box" but "out of this world". All I am doing is playing my part in reaching my community and as I and others partner together in doing that across the globe, our towns and cities begin to change, the atmosphere begins to change and there's that tipping point. And when you see that tipping point, you know that's where God wants you and faith and expectancy rise.

All the signs are that rain is coming!

ABOUT THE AUTHOR

Mark is part of the Causeway Coast Vineyard Church in Coleraine, Northern Ireland, and the founder of Healing on the Streets. Mark moved to Coleraine in 1998 with his wife Linda and their three sons.

Mark pioneered the development of the Healing on the Streets ministry, which has seen the church praying for people on the streets every week since Easter 2005. Adopted by many churches the Healing on the Streets model is spreading around the world. It is a gentle, non-confrontational way of connecting with people on the streets of our cities and introducing them to Jesus.

Mark featured in HOLY GHOST, a Darren Wilson film.

WAYS TO GET IN TOUCH...

Email us:
healing@causewaycoastvineyard.com

Or write to us at:
The Vineyard Offices
10 Hillmans Way,
Ballycastle Road
Coleraine
Co. Londonderry
BT52 2ED
Northern Ireland

Find us on Facebook:
https://www.facebook.com/healingonthestreets

Follow Mark on Twitter:
https://twitter.com/_MarkMarx